The Merchant *of* Venus

The Life of

Walter Thornton

Tile House
PUBLISHING

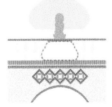

nancyn@themerchantofvenus.com

To request permissions, contact the publisher at nancyn@themerchantofvenus.com

Hardcover: ISBN ISBN: 979-8-9892735-1-5

Paperback: ISBN 979-8-9892735-0-8

Ebook: ISBN 979-8-9892735-2-2

Library of Congress Control Number: 2024903826

First paperback edition 2024

Edited by Leigh Carter

Cover art by: Adriana Thornton-Cornejo and Nancy Thornton Navarro

Photo credit: Most photos are from the private archives of Walter Thornton; some photos are in the public domain..

Facebook: https://www.facebook.com/TheMerchantofVenus

Webpage: https://themerchantofvenus.com

Tile House Publishing, LLC

Contents

Dedication

This book is a tribute to our father Walter Clarence Thornton, who secured a publishing contract for his autobiography titled "The Merchant of Venus" in 1955. Regrettably, if he did create a manuscript it remains undiscovered, a piece of history lost to time.

Additionally, we extend this dedication to our beloved mother Candelaria Thornton, whose love and care for our father endured until his last day.

Author's Note

This book is a collaboration between two daughters of Walter Thornton, a man cherished deeply by his seven children, just as he cherished them. Mr. Thornton was an exceptional individual—a combination of kindness and humor, a larger-than-life presence.

This book primarily focuses on his life before the authors were born. It presents a factual account built upon a wealth of resources, including a substantial collection of documents, photos, newspapers, magazines, books, and insightful interviews. The authors spent years meticulously researching and compiling these materials to create an accurate and thorough account of their father's life, drawing from a variety of sources with the assistance of historians and research librarians from the Library of Congress, the New York Public Library and many others from around the country.

As this is the first story of Walter Thornton's earlier life, the authors consciously chose not to overwhelm the narrative with constant citations. Instead, they have provided a carefully chosen bibliography and mention sources as the story unfolds. If you're curious to learn more about this remarkable individual or the captivating story, please feel free to contact them. Your interest is greatly appreciated.

Acknowledgments

We are deeply grateful to the wonderful individuals who have played pivotal roles in the creation of our book. Your support, dedication, and expertise have made this journey an incredible one.

Philip Mershon: Your unwavering commitment kept us on track to reach the finish line. Thank you for your invaluable contributions.

Leigh Carter: Your editing prowess and keen eye for detail have elevated our book to new heights. Your dedication to refining our work is truly appreciated.

Arlene Dahl: It is truly a remarkable stroke of fortune that the stunning and enduring icon was able to communicate with us before her passing. We will forever cherish her gracious words and the valuable insights she shared about our father.

Frankie Keane: We are profoundly grateful for your role in facilitating communication with the legendary and talented **Arlene Dahl.**

Chelsea Stone: Your research on the origins of our father's live masks, with the assistance of the pioneering female illustrator **June Tarpé Mills**, added a captivating dimension to our book. Your contributions to our narrative are immeasurable.

Librarians and Researchers: To the many librarians and researchers who guided us, we extend our heartfelt gratitude. Special thanks to Jonathan Eaker at the U.S. Library of Congress, Prints & Photographs Division.

Eric Johnson (Retired First Lieutenant of Forensic Photo Analysis Services in East Lansing, Michigan): Thank you so much for your careful analysis of the famous "bankrupt investor" photographs.

David Liston: You provided us with an unforgettable tour of the Chrysler Building, enriching our understanding and enhancing our book's content.

Tracie Townsend: As a former child model for the Walter Thornton agency and a cherished friend, your unwavering support has been a priceless asset throughout this journey.

Martin Turnbull: Your feedback, encouragement, and exceptional consultation skills greatly enhanced the quality of our book.

Dave Boarini Your priceless artistic talent and dedication to cover design and photo restoration for the book have been an dispensable contribution.

Katherine Moattar: Your wealth of marketing experience, and dedication in creating the amazing book covers, have been indispensable in promoting your grandfather's book and he is proud of you.

Stef Cornejo: Your steadfast support during the writing process at the beginning of this journey was a key factor in the success of this project. Your grandfather is proud of you.

Ivan Cornejo: Your talented skills to promote your grandfather's book with the use of photography to create videos are appreciated. Your grandfather is proud of you.

Donna Tanner: Our dear cousin, we want to express our deep gratitude for generously sharing photos from your collection and providing us with your invaluable feedback.

Kirby Kooluris: Your incredible childhood insights into your uncle's Walter life, back when we weren't even born, have been an wonderful source of information. Without you, we would have remained unaware of many details about our father's life before he moved to Mexico. We are deeply grateful for your contributions and thank you for generously sharing the numerous family photos from your collection as well.

Chapter 1

Begin Again

Nancy

We understand it's highly unusual for a man born in 1903 to have six adult children—and a widow—*all still living* as of 2024, but such is the case with our family. Our parents, Walter and Candelaria, met in Guadalajara, Mexico in 1958, when she answered a "help wanted" ad, in which he was seeking a secretary who spoke fluent English.

Our dad, Walter Thornton, was a businessman from the United States. He owned charm schools in several locations across the U.S. and Canada, and he had just moved to Guadalajara with intentions of opening his next location there. Charm schools (sometimes called finishing schools, where girls and young women were instructed in the social graces) were very big in North America and Europe in the 20th century.

Candelaria was exactly the no-nonsense kind of assistant he needed to keep him grounded. And he definitely needed grounding because a couple of things were happening that he had never counted on. The first was that the local ordinances and red tape were making the opening of his school a much slower process than an adventurous guy like my dad had bargained for. And secondly, although she was only twenty-one years old when they met and he was fifty-five, their relationship had taken the unexpected turn from business to personal and they had fallen in love.

Walter in many ways was like an impetuous kid to begin with and now with these new impediments to his business, he was losing the excitement for the new school. It occurred to him that his businesses up north were very steady and in great shape. They brought in all the money he needed to live a comfortable life. Each location had a solid management team and all that was required of him were periodic visits to each location.

He had been working hard ever since he was a preteen. Why was he wasting time trying to open another school when all he really wanted was to spend time with his new love? And so, just like that, he scrapped his plan for the school in Mexico, they were married in 1960, and Walter became a 'remote worker' long before it was common.

There then followed a progression of little Thorntons, each of us spaced almost exactly two years apart, over a twelve-year span. Our father chose our names, which were largely the first and middle names of his several siblings and parents—and himself: Walter, Jr., Roberta Virginia, Adriana Anabel, Nancy Louella, Richard Orlando and Ethel Ivette (who goes by her middle name). We were a somewhat insular, self-contained family unit. We all had friends and playmates, of course, but we relied heavily upon each other for fun and adventure.

Our beautiful mother, Candelaria, glows when she speaks about her husband, Walter. Theirs was a happy life together, for over thirty years, until he passed away in 1990. They were in love and completely involved with the living of their exciting lives in the present. The only glimpse we ever had into our father's world before us was his 'Movie Star Picture'. Well, that's what we always jokingly called it.

It was a photo from the 1920s that had been color retouched and has our dad, in profile, looking very dashing in a derby hat and a walking cane. It always sat on my mother's nightstand. Papi (as we all usually called him) dismissed it whenever we wanted to know the story behind it: "*Oh, I was just posing when this photo was taken*" with no further explanation. We all posed for photos, so we didn't ask more about it. Since we never pried further when it came to questions like this, what we eventually uncovered about Walter Thornton came as brand-new discoveries to all seven of us.

Above: Walter's movie star photo (believed to be from 1928/29)

So, how did our Ohio-born dad end up in Ajijic, Mexico, where we six Thornton kids were born and raised? Well, it was a full fourteen years after our father's passing when we were propelled to finally search for the answer to that question after a surreal, 2004 encounter with a mysterious photograph of him from 1929. What we thought would be a cursory records search has turned into a nearly two-decade journey down a phantasmagorical rabbit hole that would rival any Hollywood movie...shot in beautiful black and white.

O ld Ajijic [pronounced ah-hee-*heek*] was a kids' paradise when we were young. Picturesque mountains, canyons, Lake Chapala and the abandoned gold mines in the mountains above Ajijic, all just waiting for us to explore. There were endless opportunities for six curious little mischief-makers. A lot of our time was spent helping our parents build our castle. Yes, you read that right, *our castle*. We regularly piled into the pristine 1956, baby-blue Cadillac Coupe de Ville (our dad's pride and joy), taking trips into Guadalajara to visit its many tile factories.

The owners of the factories knew Dad by name, and vice versa. It seems likely he was one of their best, most frequent customers. He would become spellbound as he studied row after row of the beautiful, hand-painted little artworks that he would use to adorn his house, top to bottom, inside and out. It became known as his *Casa de los Azulejos* (The Tile House).

But some older, long-time residents of Ajijic still refer to it as "The Arabian Circus House," after our dad memorably invited, and hosted, a traveling circus—with multiple live elephants—to perform in our front courtyard in the early 1970s, free to all local residents. He had a standard reply when asked why he decided to cover everything in tile: "*I hate to paint.*"

Our father did base our house upon an actual blueprint by a professional architect. But the traditional, Mexican-style *casa grande* shown in the original blueprints looks absolutely nothing like the Islamic onion-domed *palacio* that our father's imagination transformed it into. He always said it was "*your mother's house. I'm building it for her.*" It was his legacy of love to the woman with whom he had found such long-sought-after happiness.

Above: Candelaria at Casa de los Azulejos April 7, 2023

I'm sure you can imagine, with a house that looked like ours, it was not uncommon for us to have perfect strangers appearing at our door, asking if they could enter the gates and have a look around, like it was a museum or a park or something. And strange as it might seem to anyone who didn't know him, I don't recall our father ever declining such a request, or saying, "*Sorry, we're busy.*" He always enjoyed giving these unannounced, guided tours. Our mother was always gracious to these drop-ins too, though with her constantly busy household, we imagine she probably would have preferred they enjoy the view of her house from the street.

Even though our dad was thirty-four years older than our mom, we really never noticed the vast age gap between them. His youthful energy was so infectious that we thought of him as ageless. And we thought of them as contemporaries to one another. Our mother is the first to admit that she never really asked him for information about his life before he met her. I remember one time about fifteen years ago pressing her for why this was the case. She answered me without mincing any words.

"I was too busy raising six kids, dogs and cats, chickens, ducks and turkeys, dealing with the construction workers and helping to build a castle to worry about what kind of life your father had when he was young. Besides, I knew your Papi had an unhappy early life. Why would I want to remind him of it? When you have six kids of your own, you'll understand. I was very busy with the present." Okay, fair enough.

The years we spent with our father leading up to his passing in 1990 were, for the most part, serene and happy times. *"When will your castle be finished?"* he'd be asked. *"I'll know it when I see it,"* he'd reply. *"But there's always room for improvement."* He did, indeed, keep making improvements, nearly all the way to the end. Though he never said as much, we think he knew that—other than his family—*Casa de los Azulejos* would be his lasting legacy in Ajijic. The castle was essentially completed on May 14, 1990, when our father was taken from us by a stroke. He had just turned eighty-seven years old.

After his passing, it was like entering a new world order for us. Normal daily events would regularly trigger memories of him. The void left by his absence seemed impossible to fill. By the same token, it very often felt as if he were still with us. He had nurtured, guided and taught us all his life lessons. His words of wisdom still ring in our ears today.

As kids we used to hang on his every word. He seemed to be an expert on, well, everything! He was the Professor of All Subjects. He also knew an endless series of corny "dad jokes": *("I failed math so many times at school, I can't even count."* or *"Before you criticize someone, walk a mile in their shoes. That way, when you do criticize them, you're a mile away and you have their shoes.")*. He was always looking for the laugh, even when it was not a laughing occasion (like, in church).

Above: (L) Walter and Candelaria 1969. (L to R) Nancy (2) Adriana (4) Richard (3 months) Roberta (6) Walter Jr. (8) (R) 1975 Richard (6) Nancy (8) Ivette (4)

Our families' lives and careers, of course, went on in the decade and a half after our father's passing. We each, individually relocated to the United States. Even our mom moved up to help with her growing brood of grandchildren and leased out the castle, furnished.

Regardless of all that change, Papi was never far from our thoughts; waking or sleeping. We all report Walter Thornton dreams. In fact, we would continue to receive visits from him in the unlikeliest of places. As you will soon see....

Chapter 2

Why is Papi in Seabiscuit?

Adriana

C hristmas Day 2004 was a special one for us. My husband, Luis, and I would be hosting the festivities at our home in Orange County, CA. Our mother, Candelaria, and three of the six Thornton siblings (and their families) were gathered under the same roof for the first time in quite a while. We'd spent most of Christmas week in my kitchen, preparing our traditional family dishes.

Our father had always been painstakingly specific about the exact ways the American staples were supposed to be prepared. Papi had largely assimilated the traditions and cuisine of Mexico, his adoptive land...though not its language (*"Why is the spoon a lady and a fork a gentleman? I'll never get it."*), but he was absolutely insistent that Thanksgiving and Christmas be traditionally American, from soup to dessert. When he told us about his life as a homeless orphan, we figured it must be important to him to enact the traditions of the happy, American family—occasions that had been in short supply during his younger days.

The piles of festively wrapped presents had grown nearly as tall as our Christmas tree. It was our fourteenth Christmas without our father, though he was never far from our thoughts or reminiscences. Most of our shared stories involved Papi and most of them involved something funny—such as his misadventures with his honeybee colony he'd fostered on the roof of the castle. Or the time when we were all out to dinner at La Posada de Ajijic and the beautiful lady came up to our dad and, with tears in her eyes, kissed his hand—right in front of our mother! We recall it happening in the late 1970s, so we were quite young, and we had *no* idea what was going on!

"Why was that lady crying, Papi?" I remember asking him.

"I guess she was glad to see me," he said, sounding as baffled as the rest of us.

"Do you know her?" I asked him.

"Not a clue," he said. *"She said she worked with me in New York."*

Our mother had flown into John Wayne Airport in Orange County to spend the holidays at my house. Nancy and her family weren't able to join us that year, since she and her husband, Art, were running their busy law practice in Dallas. That Christmas evening of 2004, after all the presents were opened and the kitchen was somewhat restored, we continued our family tradition of gathering in the living room to watch a movie. We had an enormous, pre-digital, flat-screen TV; the kind that was contained within a very tall, pressed-wood cabinet.

I arranged the seating, so that all nine of us would have optimal viewing for that year's Christmas night featured film, *Seabiscuit* (2003), which I thought our mother would enjoy, and which had recently been released on DVD. It seemed harder every year to find a film that would appeal to both kids and adults—and this one, from what I'd heard and read, seemed to be a fairly safe choice for family holiday viewing. It told the true tale of the underdog, competitive racehorse Seabiscuit, whose grit, drive and come-from-behind victories made him something of a folk hero for Depression-weary Americans in the late 1930s.

Our family tradition was for the adults to drink our *rompope* as we watched our annual Christmas entertainment. It is the Mexican version of eggnog, which we always served in special ceramic cups that only came out once a year. I did a "last call" in case anyone needed anything and then: lights out. The movie began.

Collapsing onto our large, overstuffed sofa, it felt as if it was the first time I'd actually sat down in about three days. I lay back and sank into the film's narrative, *rompope* in hand. A narrator kept the action moving as a series of vintage photographs from the early twentieth century crossed the screen. When the plot advanced to the stock market crash of 1929 and the Great Depression that followed, we got a full frame of a photograph that actually made some of us gasp in recognition—most of all, our mother.

"¡Ese es Walter!" our mother exclaimed, utterly astonished at suddenly seeing her late husband's image in a modern Hollywood movie—on Christmas Day, no less. *"Este es el mejor regalo de Navidad que podria pedir"* (This is the best Christmas gift I could have asked for), she said. As for me, it truly did feel like some kind of *Nuestra Señora de Fátima*-type of vision. It was so utterly unexpected, and I was so exhausted at that point, that I couldn't quite process this sudden appearance by our father. "Stunned" would best describe my reaction.

"Go back!" I nearly shrieked at my husband, Luis, who was controlling the remote. He did, freeze-framing the luminous photo of our handsome young father. The photo on the screen showed a fellow wearing a sporty derby hat, with his foot on the running board of a very fancy, very old car that had a big sign on it. We didn't really give thought to the big sign at first glance. We were all just completely transfixed by this

shocking image of our father, grandfather, father-in-law and husband, suddenly appearing before us in a movie (in profile just like the picture on our mother's nightstand) fourteen years after his passing!

We reversed and freeze-framed the photograph repeatedly. The kids in the room didn't really grasp what all the hubbub was about and just wanted to get back to watching the movie. But the rest of us were so completely undone at what we'd just seen, there was no possible way we could go back to concentrating on a story about some horse. We all had, more or less, the same question: Why is Papi in *Seabiscuit?*

I needed to speak to Nancy right away. I glanced at the clock and ran to a quiet part of the house to phone her. To show you how rattled I was, I did the time zone conversion in the wrong direction. I thought it was 10:30 p.m. in Texas, when in fact it was 2:30 a.m. She'd had a very long day herself, hosting Christmas dinner and festivities for her Texas clan. I just knew that she would want to know about this latest *visita*, no matter what time it was. After watching the *Seabiscuit* scene for what seemed like the four hundredth time, I'd really worked myself up. I had so many questions.

"Hello?" Nancy croaked, clearly roused from a deep slumber.

"Have you talked to anyone about Seabiscuit yet?" I asked, trying to remain calm.

"You mean the movie? What about it? Do you know what time it is here? Can't this wait until tomorrow?" Nancy replied, understandably cranky.

"No, it can't! I guess you haven't heard. Papi is in the movie!" I said.

"What? How can Papi be in Seabiscuit? *It's a new movie, right?"* she asked, suddenly very much wide awake.

"Yes, there's a very old photograph of him in the movie," I tried to explain. *"He looks very young, and it says that he was an investor or something who lost everything in the stock market crash of 1929. It was so bad that he had to sell his car for one hundred dollars on the street!"*

"That's crazy! How much rompope did you guys have? Are you sure that it's him?" Nancy asked.

"It is definitely him. Mami noticed it first. No doubt. One hundred percent sure," I replied.

"But...I don't understand. The movie says he went broke?" she asked.

"No, he is standing next to a sign on a car that says he lost everything in the stock market," I explained.

"I need to see this for myself. Where in the movie does he appear?" she asked.

"Not far into it...about fifteen minutes in," I said. *"Let's talk tomorrow...go back to sleep,"* I told her jokingly, knowing that I'd surely jolted her wide awake. *"You'll see for yourself—it is totally him."*

Not a creature was stirring by the time I got off my call to Nancy. I went back downstairs and sat, by myself, in the dark, directly in front of the enormous TV screen. I cued to the scene yet again, finally freeze-framing upon our father's image. I watched the scene one more time, as if beseeching my departed father for some kind of explanation as to how he ended up in *Seabiscuit*.

I was now really studying the sign on the car for the first time. It read: **"$100 WILL BUY THIS CAR. MUST HAVE CASH. LOST ALL ON THE STOCK MARKET."** What does that even mean? It was so confusing to me. I slow-scanned through until the end of the movie, hoping to find any kind of explanation as to why his photo suddenly appears in the film, or to see if any other images of our dad appeared. There were none; only this one.

The car was clearly a high-end, expensive car. I wondered who the other men in the photo were. I also noticed the wet sidewalk; it appeared to be slightly raining in the photo which seemed to make his circumstances even more unfortunate. Not only did he have to sell his fancy car on the street for one hundred dollars ($1750 today according to the 2023 Consumer Price Index or CPI), it was raining; and he appeared to be the only man in the image who was caught in the rain without an overcoat or umbrella.

I also remember thinking it was pretty admirable that our dad got all dressed up for this public spectacle. Instead of going the pathetic route, he decided to really "put on the dog," as he used to call it, for his grand finale on Wall Street. Driving gloves and all. His outfit certainly doesn't say "MUST HAVE CASH" but it did seem like something our father would have done—go out in style.

"If there's nothing you can do about it, you just have to hold and roll until it's over, and, at all costs, maintain your sunny demeanor," he used to say. If it was taken right after the market crash, he would have been only twenty-six in the photo. Was he a stockbroker? Or was he just an investor? Did he actually work on Wall Street? And is that where the photo was taken?

Each question led to more questions because the visual completely conflicted with the advice he had always given to us, which was to keep our personal problems "within the family." *"Keep your cards close to your vest,"* he'd say. How trapped he must have felt to have to air his proverbial "dirty laundry" so visibly.

Nancy called me back the following evening.

"Believe it or not, there's a little movie theater just a few blocks from our office, and the film they're showing is Seabiscuit, for the holidays. Art and I went to a six o'clock showing. We just got home...and I don't even know what to say," she said. *"I knew the picture was coming up, but I couldn't help but gasp when it appeared."*

"So, what did you think of it?" I asked.

"I don't know what I think!! I mean, that is absolutely him in the photograph!" Nancy exclaimed. *"But...I'm totally confused as to why this picture of him suddenly appears. Where did this picture even come from?"* she asked.

None of us really knew much of *anything* about Walter Thornton's life before his permanent move to Mexico in 1958. I mean, he would occasionally refer to his harsh childhood, but that was the only era of his life he mostly spoke to us about. And even that was usually mentioned only as a classic "dad rebuke" along the lines of "*You think your childhood is so horrible? Well, when I was your age...*" He rarely directly discussed with us the rest of his former life or career, other than through oblique, unexplained comments and observations. many of which we were unable to decipher at the time he made them. But as the puzzle pieces began to merge, many years later, we were able to recall them and finally make sense of them.

The existing remnants of our father's business and personal materials were on the grounds of the castle in Ajijic. In addition to the main part of the castle, there are a couple of separate semi-attached *casitas*. One has a round front room that includes a bath. There is a sort of mezzanine or loft area in it, accessible only with a ladder. This loft area acted in the same way for us as an attic would in a traditional American house. It was the place where things went to die.

Things that you couldn't bear to get rid of but things you really didn't want to see anymore. And you know how it goes: "out of sight, out of mind". I honestly don't think we kids, or our mother, even really knew what all was up there, and so it had gone unexplored for the fourteen years that had elapsed between our father's passing and "The *Seabiscuit* Incident" (as my family refers to that Christmas night in 2004). But seeing that car photo seemed like it was now time to finally dig into our father's personal effects.

As you might imagine, being schooled in Mexico, no one in my family was particularly well-versed on the 1929 New York stock market crash, though we'd been taught the most elementary timeline: that it caused the Great Depression of the 1930s, and that, basically, everyone in the United States became poor, overnight.

As I pondered the whole scenario even further, I realized that even if he had been a bankrupt investor in 1929, there was no great shame in that. If he lost all his money that day, so what? *Didn't everybody?* Nancy and I decided there was no question about it: We had to find out exactly what this photo was all about.

Little did we know that it would launch us on a near-twenty-year odyssey, during which we would piece together the truly stunning news that our father had been a top player in the New York scene and, by extension, Hollywood glamour. His was a life lived at the very top tier of show-business success and international fame. What we would uncover is the, until now, unexplored (and never completely documented) story of Walter "The Merchant of Venus" Thornton—parts of which read almost like a fairy tale—witches, ogres and all.

Chapter 3

Return to the Castle

Adriana

"**D**on't believe everything you read." That was one saying we heard often from our dad. "*Just because it's in print does not make it true,*" he'd say. As we started research into the life and career of our father (via the internet of early 2005) we came to understand those words as a mystical forewarning now useful to us after fifteen years since our father's passing. And we certainly were not believing everything we read, though often in a different way, as in, "*I cannot believe what I am reading about him!*"

We've made every effort to think clearly and open-mindedly in our research, to question *everything* and then proceed accordingly. Otherwise, the oncoming tidal wave of information (and misinformation) about this mysterious figure we were facing for the first time would have been almost incomprehensible. We actually needed to try to think of this "bankrupt investor" character as someone other than our father, so that we could remain unbiased in our judgments and conclusions (which also informs our alternating mentions of our father by his name, rather than as "father," "dad" or "papi").

After a conversation with our mother, she recalled that when she went to work for our dad, there had been a storage closet in their office that was full of boxes. She had never looked inside them. They didn't pertain to the day-to-day operation of the office, and Papi had told her she didn't have to be concerned with them. Everything from the office wound up in the mezzanine storage area of the *casita* at the castle, she said.

"*We need to go through Papi's papers,*" Nancy said, with a sense of urgency in her voice, when she phoned me early one morning in the spring of 2005. "*When are you next going to Ajijic,*" she asked, "*because I want to meet you there.*"

"*I was planning to go at some point this summer—but I think I need to do it sooner than that, to see what's in those boxes,*" I replied. "*Do you want to just pick a day?*"

"*How about three weeks from today? It's a three-day weekend,*" Nancy suggested. "*I'm having trouble focusing on anything but Papi at this point,*" she said. "*I'm going to take a long weekend, Friday through Sunday. Is there any way you could join me there?*" she asked, obviously understanding the utter impracticality of her request *and* the probability that I'd make it work.

"*Let me check...I'll call you back,*" I said.

Nancy and I have always had a strong sisterly bond. We've shared a spirit of adventure, too, so it wasn't unheard of for us to hop on a plane and meet somewhere, if only just to spend time together. We were usually paired in the family pecking order, since we were the two middle kids, born just two years apart. We were *como dos gotas de agua* (like peas in a pod) as we would have said it when we were kids.

I felt compelled to join her. I shared her need to start our research dive for real, right then. We both booked flights that arrived in Guadalajara on that Friday afternoon. The nice couple that was leasing the castle from our mother was aware we'd be coming down, and that we would need to access the storage area in the *casita*.

Who was this man? It felt no less strange than discovering our father had a secret, identical twin brother, or something. It still boggles our collective mind that our father was able to keep his amazing, untold life to himself all those years.

This may seem strange to those who grew up in the age of technology, but the pre-digital crowd will understand. Before everyone had a world of research at the touch of a keyboard, family history and lore were relegated to just what the elders wanted you to know...and no more. In other words, experiences of their past which didn't jive with the image they were presenting to their children, or painful memories or, God forbid, skeletons in the closet, just never got passed on. These were the pieces of the past that they 'took to the grave'. And, as for the kids of that era, they were too busy playing outside, having endless telephone calls with friends from school, and listening to records to care all that much about family histories.

We rented a small, white, Ford compact and drove the short distance from the Guadalajara airport to the castle in Ajijic. We experienced the wave of emotion we always felt upon returning home, especially since our little village had grown so enormously since our childhood there. This once fairly sleepy village was now one of the largest expatriate communities in the world—mostly consisting of American and Canadian "snowbird" refugees and retirees.

As we pulled into the lush, beautifully landscaped, tropical gardens of our neighborhood, Upper La Floresta, and into the courtyard of *Casa de los Azulejos*, it felt very strange to be seeing it as visitors, with no Thorntons in residence. This was our first visit to the castle as guests. The current residents greeted us warmly in the courtyard.

"*So nice to see you,*" the husband of the couple said. "*If there's any way we can help, just let us know. We put a ladder in the* casita *for you, just as you asked. This is a magical place and we love it here,*" he said. "*It took us a while to adjust to the tourists ringing the doorbell all the time, but we're used to it now.*"

"*It's comforting to us to know that our mother's castle is in good hands,*" I said, "*and when we were kids, those tourists used to drive us crazy, so we get it. We kids would hide whenever the doorbell rang!*"

"*Okay, I'll confess: We've done the same thing!*" said the current lady of the house, laughingly.

We had both brought flashlights as the windowless loft was quite dark. Up we went. It wasn't difficult to isolate the boxes of Papi's stuff from all the other boxes that contained old family medical records and things like school report cards from when we were kids. In all, there were eleven boxes and one oversized green leather bag.

"Why do I feel like I'm going to get in trouble for looking at this stuff?" Nancy said.

I felt the same way. It was equal parts scary and exciting.

We formed a two-person "bucket brigade"—one in the loft to hand boxes down, one halfway up the ladder to receive them and put them next to a large table that was going to be our workspace. Once everything was down, we lugged a big leather bag up onto the table, unzipped it and, looking in, discovered eight-by-ten photographs and press clippings. Thousands of them! We looked at each other, our eyes bugged out, and we started removing the bag's contents by the fistfuls, putting things into piles on the desktop.

We created a tabletop filing system, in which we tried to broadly categorize what we were finding. We printed signs for the piles: Car Photo, Childhood, Newspapers and Magazines, Modeling, and Legal (One of his boxes contained strictly business and legal papers, which we decided to keep boxed and save for later.) Surprisingly, our "Car Photo" pile remained empty.

Mind you, it's not as if the contents of our father's records were in any kind of chronological order, or filed in any way at all—so what we were uncovering appeared before us in an utterly disordered fashion. There he was in the U.S. Army, during World War I. There he was, standing next to Bob Hope at the 1939 New York World's Fair. Then there was an eleven-inch-by-thirteen-inch formal, sepia portrait of him, marked 1926, in which he looked like a green-eyed version of Rudolph Valentino in the style of the "Latin Lover" with his slicked-back hair reflecting the light.

We later researched the credited photographer of the "Latin Lover" portraits— "Irving Chidnoff, NY." He was a well-known celebrity photographer in the 1920s and 30s. His catalog of portraits included many of the top Broadway and Hollywood stars of the late 1920s: Gloria Swanson, Marion Davies, Jean Harlow, John Barrymore, Marlene Dietrich, Bette Davis—and many others. Walter was only twenty-three when his photo was taken. In the profile shot, his clear, green eyes appear almost translucent, as he gazes toward a distant light.

Above: Twenty-three-year-old Walter Thornton, 1926 (Portrait by Irving Chidnoff)

Our father's former life was fanned out before us, with glimpses of various facets of an extraordinary earlier life that he had kept entirely to himself. The question we kept repeating after each of our surprise discoveries: *Why didn't he tell us about this?*

"*Put that one on the 'important' pile,*" Nancy said. We'd both arrived with large, mostly empty suitcases, knowing we'd likely be taking the "important" pile back home with us—and that pile turned into five growing piles of things we needed to explore in much greater depth.

"*This clipping calls him 'The Star Maker' and lists the stars that he made,*" I pointed out. "*Lizabeth Scott, Cathy Downs, Susan Hayward and Arlene Dahl.*"

As we continued slicing open the long-sealed boxes, it became truly overwhelming, the sheer volume of information we had on our hands that pertained to music, mannequins, bathing suits, newspaper columns, radio show info, TV show info and more —and we only had about a day and a half in which to go through it. Focus, focus!

By the time we opened the tenth and final box (excepting business records), both Nancy and I were practically numb to the multiple mysteries we were uncovering, yet, *still* we found no mention of the "bankrupt investor" image—or any reference to our dad having "lost all." In fact, quite the opposite. So in finding absolutely nothing in our father's papers regarding the market crash photo, we had to put our thinking about it aside for a while. It had to go in the growing file of "Mysteries to Solve."

And just like his 'filing system' in the boxes, it wasn't as if we learned our father's story in any sort of linear fashion. It seemed as if the story of Walter Thornton had a new, surprising discovery at every turn. It was like reading a book with the chapters out of order.

It's hard to remember now just *what* we thought of the car photo at that point. What I do know is, back then we trusted that what we were seeing in the image was the truth, a biographical depiction of our father's economic collapse. Why would we have thought otherwise? No, that early on we had not yet taken into account that a sinister act of sabotage might factor into the equation.

B y Saturday evening, after a day and a half of non-stop digging through the boxes, we needed to sit down and assess what we'd just uncovered. Nancy suggested we have dinner at our hotel restaurant, which was just above the *Malecón de Ajijic*, the beautiful lakefront promenade downtown. We had taken adjacent rooms at the plush La Nueva Posada de Ajijic hotel for our stay. Again, it felt very strange to be visiting our hometown as tourists, but this hotel felt a little bit like home to us, since it had prominently featured in our childhood.

I'd made a 7 p.m. reservation for two under "Thornton." At that time, the main restaurant in the hotel was called La Rusa, in honor of Ajijic's most eccentric resident, the late Zara Alexeyewa—known locally by all as "La Rusa" (the Russian Lady—who was actually from Brooklyn). We instantly recognized the man behind the bar, Jose Martinez-Toriz, who was known to all as *Guero Jamaicon* ("The Blond Jamaican," and though he and his family were blond, they were not Jamaican). He was a suave, handsome man who'd bartended at the original Posada for years, before following the owners to La Rusa in 1990. When I think of him, I always envision him with a cocktail shaker in mid-shake, next to his head.

"*Buenas tardes, señoras,*" he said in his polished, professional demeanor. "*Bienvenidas a La Rusa. ¿Van ha cenar con nosotros está noche?*" But in the midst of delivering his welcome, he suddenly recognized both of us, even though we hadn't seen him in several years.

"*Señor Toriz! I am Adriana and this is Nancy Thornton,*" I interrupted, giving in to my urge to give him a big hug. "*I guess we've changed a little since you last saw us.*"

"Por supuesto, *of course you are! I remember all of you Thorntons,*" he said. "*I always remember what a beautiful family you were. One of you Thornton sisters represented La Posada in the Miss Chili Cook-Off contest one year, didn't you?*" he asked.

"*Yes, that was me, Nancy. One of my prizes was a trip to California—and I decided to stay in the U.S.,*" she said.

"*Well, that explains why we haven't seen you in a while,*" he said. "*I saw your reservation in the book and thought we would be seeing Candelaria or your brother, Walter Junior, tonight.*" "*No, it's just the two of us,*" I said. "*We're only here until tomorrow.*"

"*Well, then we had better make this special!*" Señor Toriz said, leading us into La Rusa.

Ajijic's tastiest sangria was served there as some restaurants served water, *gratis.*

Raising her glass heavenward, Nancy said, "*This is to you, Walter Thornton. We're looking for you, Papi.*" We both had early flights the next morning and by this point in our weekend dig, we were both a bit brain-fogged from the overwhelming amount of information we'd just faced for the first time. Where to begin? We each brought to the restaurant a few selected items from Papi's papers, to discuss over dinner. We placed them on the table, far away from the pitcher of sangria.

"*Well, I don't know about you, but the first thing I want to find out is how did Papi go from being a homeless orphan to becoming a famous model and later a top modeling agent practically overnight?"* I said. *"It's as if he'd made the leap from being a street kid to becoming this world-famous beauty expert in something like ten-years' time. How did he do that?"*

"I know! Just from what we've read so far, he was this world-renowned, go-to-guy on beauty!" Nancy replied. *"And he had so many titles... The Merchant of Venus... The Model King... The Pin-Up King... The Star Maker... The Profile,"* she said, still somewhat awestruck by our discoveries. *"And I guess he must have gone bankrupt in the stock market in the middle of it, somehow,"* she said, perfectly echoing my own confusion on that matter. Boy, did we have so much to learn.

Señor Toriz returned to our table, once we'd settled in. *"We're truly honored to have you back here with us tonight. Your father was a great, great gentleman,"* he said, humbly. *"Everyone in Ajijic knew of your parents, and even though he's been gone for many years, we still remember him at La Nueva Posada,* "he continued, *"which is why tonight, your dinner is* en la casa. *It is the least we can do for the family of our friend, Walter Thornton."*

"Gracias," I replied. It was so touching to hear our father was still so well-remembered, all these years later. As we got back down to the topic at hand Nancy said, *"So, we didn't find the car image in the boxes. Do you think it was sort of a secret from his past that he wanted to keep hidden and forget?"* *"I've found nothing about him failing, anywhere,"* I replied. *"All I'm finding is information on what a huge success he was in 1929, and beyond."*

"Exactly... it makes no sense," Nancy replied.

So, our first motivator in trying to uncover our father's unknown first life—that picture—became a stumbling block and would remain so for several more years. The answer would turn out to be a shocker. We would eventually exhaust all resources in trying to find the answers to the many riddles behind the "bankrupt investor" image—employing the Library of Congress, the New York Public Library, declassified FBI documents, forensic photographic analysis, as well as every viable research outlet we could find. Not to mention the limitless wealth of information—both false and true—on the World Wide Web.

We ultimately gathered enough fact-based information that our father was not, in fact, a bankrupt stock market investor. Or even a successful stock market investor. We uncovered no proof that our father had been *any* kind of active "player" in the stock market at all, at any point in his life. But it would take us another decade and a half of solid research before we reached our own conclusions as to what on earth was going on in that "bankrupt investor" image.

Chapter 4

A Homeless Orphan

Nancy

Walker Thornton, a barber (1870-1904) and his wife Virginia Louella (1871-1914) lived in a tiny, speck-on-the-map town of Beaver, Ohio in a log cabin. After the birth of their first three children, Elsie Roberta (known as Betty), Ethel and Wilbur, they welcomed the birth of their last child, Walter, on April 3, 1903. Walter would never really know his father, Walker, who died a year later from tuberculosis.

With four young mouths to feed, Louella soon married again to the man who would become Walter's stepfather, John Lee. John was a farmer, and the new family settled onto his small farm in Chillicothe, Ohio, a farming town in the Appalachian foothills and once the capital of Ohio. There they would have three more children: Beatrice, Irene and William.

Walter attended school except when he was needed on the farm, when all hands pitched in at harvest time. Occasionally he would save up a few pennies to visit the little candy store near the bridge by his house. Evidently Walter stood out from all the other kids who came to the store because when he came back to visit Chillicothe at age twenty, after close to a decade away, the elderly shop owner remembered him by name. It wasn't a surprise to us that Dad had a way with women even at that age. He made sure to always sweet-talk the shop lady just to brighten her day.

Unfortunately, Louella followed Walter's father to the grave from the same disease when Walter was only eleven years old. And Louella had been the glue that held the family together throughout good times and bad. Upon her death, the Thornton-Lee family splintered apart. Betty (eighteen at the time) and Ethel (just sixteen) were both married that spring. Beatrice and Irene, Walter's younger half-sisters were adopted into separate families. William remained with his father, while Wilbur went north to Canada, which had just entered WWI, and joined the military as a minor.

In the numerous interviews Walter gave over the years, he never told the tabloids that he was actually abandoned by his older sister Betty at the railroad station in Chillicothe. Betty told him to wait for her. He waited for many hours and she just never came back. Her new husband, Charlie, was the influence on that maneuver that would mark Dad's life forever. Walter was left alone to look after himself.

Eventually, Walter was taken off the streets and placed in an orphanage that was like something out of Dickens. His admonition to us as kids was, "*If you don't knock that off, I'm going to shave all your heads!*" This was either one of many punishments handed out at the orphanage or it might have been to prevent the spread of head lice. After a few months of that living hell, he escaped at the age of twelve.

Unfortunately, he was soon captured and indentured into a farm work-camp, which was run by a cruel and violent married couple who wouldn't even allow our dad to sleep indoors—even in the freezing winter months. He eventually escaped from there as well and set off on a nomadic existence with no destination in mind. He got by on his own wits and resources, mostly sheltering in barns and other farm outbuildings.

I recall a story that had made such a vivid impression upon me that he told us when we were on one of our hikes not far from our house. It was a very hot day. We stopped under a small grove of shade trees and opened the picnic basket our mother had prepared for us. Our dad stood next to a fencepost, where he placed his chin on top of the crook of his arm on the post. He appeared lost in his thoughts, focusing upon a small herd of cows grazing nearby.

"Did you know that if you sleep next to a cow, she will never get up before you do?" he asked us. *"She will stay next to you until you get up."*

"How do you know that, Papi?" our sister, Roberta asked him.

"Because for a while there, that was where I used to sleep...in barns, in open fields. Out in the Ohio farm country during winter, a cow was the closest source of heat you were going to find—other than making your bed beneath the resting train locomotives that arrived at Chillicothe Station. The stationmaster used to let me sleep under the parked, still-warm locomotives sometimes. But mostly, during the winter, I slept between the cows. They took care of me. They're very gentle creatures, cows are," he explained. *"They were my only friends for a while there."*

He also vividly related tales of delivering typewriters to rural locations, on foot, at age twelve. In 1915, typewriters were extremely heavy. He'd recall trudging through waist-high snowbanks, delivering cumbersome typewriters in sub-freezing weather. We always assumed he was joking—that he exaggerated his childhood circumstances for dramatic effect. Eventually we confirmed: He did not exaggerate. If anything, he underplayed the dire severity of his entire youth.

I remember a conversation I had with my dad once, on the topic of good deeds. *"Do you want to talk about kindness?"* he asked. *"One Christmas Eve when I was a young kid, I was having a really rough time. I'd escaped from the orphanage. I had nowhere to live. I slept on the streets in and around Chillicothe, Ohio. It was snowing like crazy and it was ungodly freezing. I guess I must have looked in pretty tough shape. I didn't have shoes, other than the ones I'd made myself, out of corrugated cardboard and rope, because I had outgrown my only real pair of shoes. Almost sent from Heaven, a wonderful old couple stopped me and said, 'Son, are you warm enough? Why aren't you with your family?'*

"I told them I didn't have any family and that my parents were dead. The lady said, 'Then can we get you a pair of shoes for Christmas?' And they did. They marched me directly to my very first men's shoe store. Even though I was only about twelve, it seemed like my feet grew before

the rest of me did, practically overnight, and regularly. I walked out of there in a sturdy pair of leather, lace-up work boots, with room to grow.

"Two pairs of woolen socks, too. They also gave me a silver half-dollar coin and wished me 'Merry Christmas.' They were the only two people who wished me 'Merry Christmas' that year. Their kind deed has always stayed with me...and that happened in 1915.

Woodrow Wilson was the president. All these years later, I still think about that couple. If it hadn't been for them, your old Dad would probably have no toes right now. So, never forget: The simplest kind deed can change someone's life. The ancient Greek philosopher Aristotle said, 'Virtue is its own reward' which is a fancy way of saying the very fact that you're doing a kind deed, even if you don't get thanked for it, should be reward enough."

"Remember when he used to give coins and candy to the kids on the street on his daily walks to the Ajijic plaza?" I reminded Adriana.

"Yes," she said. *"I was so jealous that one day I took all the candy to my room and ate as much as I could and got really sick."*

"We were such little brats back then," I said, and we both laughed.

A homeless orphan. Is it even possible to have a worse start in life than that? Where did he get this otherworldly wisdom regarding everything related to beauty? Not to mention the determination to press forward so aggressively with his business plan? And at such a young age. When we contemplated these questions, we continued to be astonished by his leaps-and-bounds trajectory.

His schooling after the age of eleven had been sporadic, at best. He didn't attend high school, college or university. But really, is defining and marketing a world of beauty something that can even be taught? Or is it possible that a "sense of beauty" is like any of the other human senses, like an especially acute sense of taste or hearing? Whatever was the case, Walter Thornton catapulted to the head of the pack. How did he do that? He once said in *The New True Story Magazine*, January 1940 article:

"I was both a model and a sculptor. For a brief time I acted in motion pictures, during the silent days. This background has served me in good

stead, not only in judging beauty but in the more important phase, helping the girls I manage, to get the greatest effect out of their natural endowments."

Seventy-five percent of all movies from the silent era are considered 'lost'. And even though we haven't found contracts or discovered any credits on IMDb, he was listed in the John Robert Powers *Actors' Directory & Studio Guide* in 1927. We have found photographs that looked like they were shot on a movie set. We are still hoping to find a film with him in it.

Above: Photos of Walter Thornton that appear to be taken while acting in silent films

We found out that our dad, unimaginably, had enlisted in the U.S. Army when he was fourteen, just like his brother did in the Canadian Army. *"Wow...look at this...it's a photo of Papi when he was in the Army,"* Adriana exclaimed. *"He looks like a baby here, he is so young."* It had a hand-written, penciled inscription on the back that said, "PFC Walter C. Thornton, World War, 1917." We confirmed that when this photo was taken, he was exactly fourteen-and-a-half years old.

Above: Private First-Class Walter Clarence Thornton, 1917

We found a piece of correspondence from this time to his older sister, Betty. Even after being left at the train station by her, Walter couldn't sever ties with her and seemed to understand that she was just doing her husband's bidding. Since Walter had been drifting the past few years, she didn't even know where he was until this breezy update letter arrived from him, which sent her into a flurry of corrective action. Put another way, Betty freaked out.

On April 2, 1917, the day before Walter's fourteenth birthday, President Woodrow Wilson declared war upon Germany, launching The Great War (later known as World War I). Piecing together her correspondence with the U.S. Army, we figured out it was Aunt Betty who'd busted Walter. Literally hours before he was set to ship out to Europe from New Jersey, Betty was able to get the U.S. Army to yank him from duty. She did the same thing with his brother, Wilbur, who was only sixteen. He had fully enlisted in the Canadian Army and had already shipped off to France.

Betty let the military authorities in Canada know that Wilbur was underaged, too. Both Thornton brothers were called back from service. Betty had been out of her brothers' lives since the family scattered after their mother's death in 1914. And perhaps due to guilt at leaving her younger brothers behind, sister Elsie Roberta "Betty" Thornton Goetz snapped to attention and provided some timely, sisterly intervention for those boys.

The letter that ended Private Thornton's military career began, *"Dear Sister Betty."* It went on:

I am up here in Gettysburgh getting along fine... the Army is the only place for a working man.

We have our exercise up here and the drilling is fine. it certainly makes a man out of you.

I have a good uniform & gun & everything I need so I should [not] worry about the cold weather. I just got a letter from Ethel & Ted (and he) is making $80 per month... that is better than he has done yet, if he hangs onto it. I'm going to buy a Liberty Bond and see how much I can save. Well, as it is getting late, I will close for this time. Hoping to hear from you soon.

Your Brother Walter

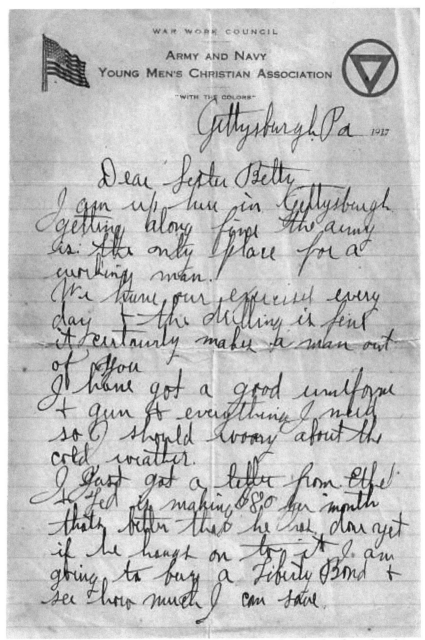

Above: Walter's tidy, cursive handwriting belies the fact that his formal education ended at the age of eleven. Ethel and Ted were Walter's (and Betty's) older sister and her husband.

After he was discharged from the army, we believe he may have been living with his older brother Wilbur for several years when they were not much more than latchkey kids. He eventually made his way to New York where he stayed very briefly with the Goetzes who lived in a flat at 507 West 186th Street, in the northern section of Manhattan known as Washington Heights.

"*He sometimes talked about being in the Army, but I always assumed he meant World War II. Nineteen seventeen was WWI,*" I said. How does a fourteen-year-old even enlist in the U.S. Army?

Chapter 5

The Ideal, Jazz Age Young Man Model

Adriana

I t wouldn't be that great a stretch to call the discovery of Walter Thornton sort of a progenitor of all modern-day, show-business "overnight discovery" stories. Launched to instant, show-business success while repairing brickwork in the park? That kind of stuff doesn't really happen...does it? Well, unlikely as it sounds, it did happen to our father, when he was just twenty-two years old.

We got the story from Myra Dolan, who worked as a manager at the agency from the mid-1930s to the early 1950s and also happened to be our dad's sister-in-law. Later on, we managed to find evidence to back up the tale, including newspaper articles and profiles. One particularly interesting piece was from a 1931 edition of the *New York Daily Mirror*, written by a columnist named Jack Lait. We also pieced together more details from personal letters and documents we found in the boxes. These pieces of the puzzle helped us fill in the gaps and tell the story of our dad's "discoverer," who turned out to be a beautiful young artist.

A twenty-six-year-old art student, Georgia Warren, had just begun her first year as a student/apprentice at the National Academy of Design in 1925. There had been a well-publicized, nationwide search for the six young artists who would be chosen as the very first crop of "artists-in-residence" there. She had been living in Denver when she applied for the prestigious scholarship program, which she won, much to her astonishment.

The prize included a round-trip, private-compartment train ticket, from Denver's Union Station to Pennsylvania Station—where she arrived less than three days later. As soon as she entered the grand terminal, she looked around and wondered whether she'd be able to cash in her return ticket.

Much of her days consisted of private studies with prominent artists and scholars. The remainder of her time was spent on "sketch work", working on her own paintings and other artistic disciplines. Georgia had always been particularly good at figural painting, especially capturing faces, mainly beautiful faces. And hers was one. She could often be found painting before mirrors rather than having to hire live female models.

ARTIST PRETTY ENOUGH FOR MODEL

GEORGIA WARREN

Above: (L) Artist Georgia Warren, 1929. (R) Undated photograph of Walter Thornton, thought to be from one of his earliest professional photo shoots, ca. 1925-26, just after his encounter with Georgia Warren

Her latest assignment was to paint a New York street scene...in oil. Most of Georgia Warren's experience to date had been in watercolor painting. Oil painting was an expensive medium to work in, previously beyond her means as an unknown artist, one who had other priorities—such as eating. But the terms of her scholarship covered all her canvasses and her supplies, so oil on canvas it would be.

She sat in the shade of Morningside Park, where she'd set up with a view down Columbus Avenue. It was here, just a short walk from the Academy, that she would do her initial sketch work that would be incorporated into her cityscape painting. But there, near the entrance of the park, a young bricklayer lifted pallets of bricks and pavers to the curb from a truck, next to his tub of wet concrete and his bricklayer's trowel. Something about him kept drawing her attention.

Georgia had initially planned to make the human characters in her painting almost featureless and impressionistically vague. But she found herself studying the bricklayer at work. She'd spent time studying how the tendons of his neck strained against the hod of bricks he hoisted from the truck. She thought to herself, "*That neck! That profile! Those shoulders!*" He was working by himself, repairing the broken brickwork at the entry to the park. His thin, gray work shirt was soaked through with perspiration; the sleeves were rolled up to reveal his well-developed biceps. His denim work trousers bore smears and splatters of the cement he was working with; his well-worn work boots did, too.

He had been returning to work on the same spot for the past couple days so she'd had plenty of time to covertly study his face and form from her position, just a few yards away. The more she examined him, the more she realized: This young fellow isn't just handsome—he is perfectly proportioned to be an artist's model. She couldn't get over what a flawless profile he possessed. There was an earnestness, a sincerity and a naturalness to Walter that was appealing. She thought that Walter seemed to personify the qualities of the ideal All-American Young Man, circa 1925.

Georgia was not the type of person to approach a stranger on any street, let alone in New York City, where she'd only lived for three months. But when she finished sketching out the section that included the handsome young bricklayer, she felt compelled to speak with him. Carrying her sketchbook with her, she walked over to a now-seated Walter Thornton. Introducing herself, she told him that she had included him in a sketch for a painting she would be doing. She turned the book around to reveal her rendering of the twenty-two-year-old, hoisting a pyramidal tower of bricks onto his broad shoulders. He was surprised and flattered by the rendition.

In short order, she explained that she was an apprentice at the National Academy of Design. They were always hiring models for sculptors, painters and illustrators. And, she said, in her observation as an artist, he had the perfect face and form to be an artist's model. Was this something he might consider?

Her pitch to him was at a very rapid, excited speed and, frankly, a bit dizzying. But everything slowed to absolute clarity when she reached the part where she said that in two to three days of *just standing still* he could make the equivalent of his six-day-a-week salary for hard labor! Was she kidding? Was he dreaming? He told her that he, too, wanted to be an artist, a sculptor actually, and the brickwork was just to save money so he could begin. When she asked him if he would pose for her at the Academy and, once there, she could introduce him around to other artists who frequently used models, he only had two questions: Where and when?

Walter finished his bricklaying shift at six o'clock. He couldn't wait to rush home to tell Betty what had just happened to him. This offer of a job working amongst fellow artists seemed almost too good to be true. Could this Georgia Warren lady just be fooling with him somehow? Did she have some kind of angle he wasn't detecting? His dream scenario had been to relocate himself to where the rest of the artists in New York City lived—Greenwich Village—and move into a live-in studio where he could sculpt. He would never achieve that dream while sweating over an endless pile of bricks and pavers, and he knew it. Maybe this posing for other artists thing could be his ticket out.

Walter surely hadn't set out to be a bricklayer his entire life. He knew next to nothing about bricklaying. He'd known nothing about delivering heavy typewriters or piloting a horse-drawn butcher's wagon, starting back when he was twelve, either. His life since the deaths of his parents had been an endless cycle from one manual labor job to the next.

And though sculpting was his current interest in the short term, he didn't know what he wanted to *be* for the long term. He just knew that it was time for him to start a life of his own, away from the limiting confines of a dead-end job and an overly monitored existence at his sister Betty's house. He realized it was time to move on; by himself, once again.

When Walter showed up to meet Georgia on the sidewalk in front of the National Academy of Design a couple days later, he was just as good-looking but there was also an air of self-possessed confidence. Assimilation to uncharted surroundings would prove to be a personal specialty for Walter. And so, his ascent up the front stairs into the

National Academy of Design foretold his upcoming personal ascent through a New York that would ultimately be his.

Above: Undated, mid-1920s. Snapshots of Walter Thornton modeling on Fifth Avenue

Soon after Walter's encounter with Georgia Warren, he left the Goetz home for good, moving for a few months into the West 57th Street YMCA before finally realizing his dream of moving to Greenwich Village.

In the early twentieth century, the Young Men's Christian Association offered more than just bare-bones, inexpensive, temporary lodgings and gymnastic training facilities for young men. It also featured an extensive residential curriculum of visiting lecturers and instructors who taught wholesome-minded doctrines of self-improvement. The most prominently featured lecturer at the 57th Street YMCA when Walter was there was Dale Carnegie.

Walter enrolled in sculpting classes as well as some of Carnegie's self-improvement seminars, especially those that Carnegie gave on confident public speaking. Dale Carnegie actually took an interest in Walter and his eager potential as a disciple of the Carnegie philosophy of optimism. Carnegie's popularity continued to heighten, as a roving oracle in the school of positive thought and self-improvement.

Georgia Warren's career as an artist continued to thrive. Her renderings of Hollywood stars soon graced the covers of Hollywood fan magazines that lined newsstands in the 1930s. Her works are prized today as some of the most vivid cover illustrations from the Golden Age of Hollywood.

Georgia Warren has also achieved immortal renown as a cover artist for the pulp fiction magazines of the 1930s-1950s. She has even sometimes been referred to as "The Pulp Queen." Walter Thornton never forgot the beautiful artist who had launched him on his career. He later supplied models to Georgia Warren for many years—discounted at the "family rate"—including some of his most popular later discoveries. We hope to one day find the painting that Georgia Warren made of our father.

Chapter 6

Male Subjects, Mannequins and Models

Nancy

The Greenwich Village artist's model scene of the mid 1920s that Walter moved into was a loosely defined group of mostly young students, and underemployed actors who saw the viability of cashing-in on their faces and figures by posing before artists—painters, sculptors, illustrators and lithographers—and, eventually, photographers. It was centered on and around the campus of New York University. History has framed Greenwich Village during that era as a Bohemian paradise, where free-thinking creative types found others just like them.

Walter's success in his new field was in part due to his impeccable timing, landing upon the art world of New York City at the peak of the golden age of lithography. It wasn't long after being discovered by Georgia Warren that word began to spread among artists about the young male model with the stunning profile.

Above: Photo of 22-year-old Walter, 1926, which accentuated his versatility as both a face and physique model. He honed his muscles at the 57th Street YMCA, where he also took up amateur prizefighting. (Photographer unknown)

His broad forehead, artistically proportioned nose, confidently jutting jawline and his earnest, penetrating gaze seemingly exemplified young American manhood at that moment in time. He was perfectly handsome, but not *overly* handsome. In other words, for the consumer browsing magazines for hats or suits or sportswear, he was *relatable* (the ultimate goal in the advertising world). In Walter, whatever alchemy was at play, all his features merged to create a young *everyman* image for artists to interpret.

The other great bonus for the female ad demographic was that he represented a solid, perfectly groomed, dashing, handsome and athletic young man. He posed as a dreamy bridegroom in multiple ads. This undated/unsourced photo (below) we found in our dad's papers is thought to be from 1928-929. From the excited gaggle of spectators, it appears to be from a live fashion show. All the participants appear to be models which illustrates how models came in all ages and sizes. It may also be an early example of a tradition that continues to the present: that of ending a fashion show with a fashionable bride.

Above: Walter Thornton modeling as a groom ca. 1928

Not only did Walter have a perfect profile for the artistic modeling world but he had something else. He had an undeniable charisma, and his unaffected and professional demeanor was a breath of fresh air in the pre-1930 New York art world. He was always known to be either early or exactly on time, never late. By all accounts, he was easily directable and was always collaborative, cooperative and pleasant. Walter built a name for himself through equal amounts of looks and dedicated professionalism, simple as that.

In 1926, the first year the John Robert Powers Agency represented our father, the standards of male beauty in America were very much in flux. The early 1920s Leyendecker's all-American young gods, as well as Hollywood's handsome *everyman*, Wallace Reid, were briefly sidelined by the "Latin Lover" craze of that era, as epitomized by Hollywood silent film star Rudolph Valentino. Young men on the prowl became known as "sheiks" and liberated young women as "shebas." His reign was a brief one, though, when he succumbed to a case of peritonitis in August 1926.

With the shocking death of Valentino, the "Sheik Craze" came to a halt. Fortunately for Walter Thornton, his own entry into the professional modeling world came about just as his more "all-American" looks came back into fashion. Those 'green-eyed Valentino' portraits that we mentioned earlier were shot just five months before Valentino's death.

Above: (L) 23-year-old Walter Thornton, 1926 (Portrait by Irving Chidnoff) (R) Undated promotional modeling shot, ca. 1927-28. Both from the personal effects of Walter Thornton.

The term "male model" only largely came into common usage after Walter Thornton became one of the first of them. An argument could be made that the Walter Thornton Model Agency helped popularize the very term "model," since in the 1920s, the Powers Agency referred to its models as "subjects"—male subject, female subject, child subject, or sometimes by the even starker "mannequins" or "manikins."

Most artist's male models at the time seemed to view their modeling as a passing lark, certainly not as an actual vocation. It was something to do while "between engagements" in theater and film work. In the earliest news coverage of Walter Thornton, there was an emphasis on the sheer novelty value of this "luckiest-guy-in-the-world," who makes his living *simply by being a man model!* And that was all he did once he put his acting and sculpting aside to concentrate on modeling since his popularity as a model had grown.

As we continued to read references of how many ads our father had appeared in, we systematically set out to find them. Thankfully, we were able to access the *Saturday Evening Post* and the *Vanity Fair* archived publications from 1821 and 1913 respectively. We divided the labor between us. We needed to study every issue of both magazines from 1925 to 1931, the years that encompassed our father's modeling career. Plus, all the advertisements and all the featured fictional stories, which were usually illuminated with illustrations. He was in a lot of those, too.

It's a tricky thing, trying to identify models in illustrated renderings, to say the least. Imagine trying to find one of your own parents in an artist's rendering from nearly a century ago. It is a skill that neither of us had ever been called upon to employ. But we soon got the hang of it, examining our father's perfect ears, nose, hairline and jawline. I guess we'd never considered the fact that not all illustrators created literal visions of their models. But we started coming across advertisements that indisputably featured our father. We've only "claimed" the ones that we're completely certain are him, just by our facial recognition of our dad.

"You realize we can now recognize the shape of Papi's cranium? How many daughters can make that claim?" I asked. We learned to spot the distinctive shape and placement of our father's ears, too, after studying so many professional images of him. We started another folder called "Maybe Walter," which contained the ads on which we were still inconclusive.

"Then how about this one?" Adriana said, texting one more for the "Maybe Walter" file. *"It's from a Texaco ad from March of 1929. The ears look pinned-on like Papi's,"* she said, quoting a line from an article we found. *"Such a strange way to put it. Why would ears be "pinned-on?"*

"Not sure about the first one, but the second one for sure. And talk about 'for sure,' look at this! There is no doubt about this one! I found it on eBay and it just arrived," I emailed Adriana with excited urgency.

We'd seen mentions that our dad had been known as "The Dobbs Hat Man," which is how I found a December 1927 edition of *Vanity Fair* magazine on eBay. *Vanity Fair* ran a years-long, deluxe photographic ad campaign, featuring the full-page, artistic, men-in-hats photographs of Alfred Cheney Johnston, who was considered the preeminent "portrait photographer to the stars" of the 1920s and early 1930s. He is known best today for his photographing the *Ziegfeld Follies Girls* in daring images, many of them fully nude.

To find a full-page advertisement that featured a photograph, as opposed to an illustration, from as early as 1927 is most unusual, in that photographic ads in magazines were still comparatively rare. But we had no doubts whatsoever that this was our father:

"This one goes in the "definite" pile. I love this picture of him," Adriana said. *"Such a great shot!"*

The bottom line is, within a half-year of being discovered, Walter had to turn down work with famous artists. His date book was soon filled several weeks in advance with sittings with almost every great illustrator of the early twentieth century.

Chapter 7

A Modern Adonis

Nancy

B efore we go any further, this is a good time to explain something for context, otherwise things might get confusing. To begin with, since radio was in its infancy, and not fully programmed yet (and television was still a long way off) magazines were the big thing throughout the 1920s and into the mid-1930s. They were read by everyone, everywhere. Whether you picked them up at the newsstand, the drug store or by mail via subscription, every home had stacks of them. They contained feature articles, fictional stories, multi-part serials and, most importantly, *advertising*.

The ads and the stories were visually augmented with imagery. But, up till the early 1930s anyway, most of the imagery used were illustrations rather than photographs. Don't get me wrong—photos were used, but they were used very sparingly because the technology to reproduce actual photographs in mass-market print was still very crude and *very* economically prohibitive.

It wasn't until reproduction and printing became more advanced in the early 1930s which allowed the price to come down on photo reproduction, that photo imagery became the norm. Suddenly, those few lucky illustrators who were still able to get work were in the business of creating lurid covers for pulp fiction paperbacks.

But before all that happened, illustrators in the 1920s worked a couple of different ways: either booking a live model to draw, or booking a live model to photograph and then draw from that picture. The photos in the latter case were known as a "lithographer's template" or "illustrator's template". In our dad's case, there was a third way, but let's not get ahead of ourselves.

To further illustrate this point, we found two photos in our dad's boxes that were used in April of 1930 by the famous illustrator Will Grefé, who had taken the pictures and used them to make illustrations for two different fictional stories in the *Saturday Evening Post*. One story was called "We All Know It", and appeared in the April 12 issue, and the other was, "Without Recourse", appearing in the April 19 issue. It was an amazing experience for Adriana and me to see dad's photos and then to find the actual illustrations for which they were the template.

Above: Photos of Walter Thornton and unknown female models used as illustrators' templates. Actual drawings available in the respective publications.

Fairly early in our web search into our father's former life, I came across an extraordinary, front-page profile and interview with Walter Thornton, dated August 10, 1930. It tells of Walter's life and career up to that point. This meant that it would have covered the period before and after the stock market crash. The *New York World*'s headline reads, "Bricklayer Parks Trowel; Emerges as Glorified Youth of 'Collar Ads." It presents a reliable framework for us to base our father's early timeline upon. It refers to him as "...one of the best-known young men in America." And that claim was assuredly not in relation to the stock market crash.

I called Adriana to specifically discuss the "Bricklayer" article. I'd emailed her a copy of it. *"That article is amazing,"* I said. *"He was a major, early male model; he was big-time famous!"*

You only need to read this portion of the article to see what a wild success our dad was by the summer of 1930:

"Walter Thornton is one of the best-known young men in America. That is, everybody knows his face, but few know his name. You can't take a ride in the river without seeing his smile and his features between you and the landscape. (This refers to the advertisements that were everywhere on ferryboats.) You see him a dozen times a day in the street cars. He literally is everywhere. Turn to almost any page of any magazine and there he is. You can't escape him.

"He is the young man who is famous for his nonchalance in each and every situation. He is the young man who became the life of the party because he had learned to play the saxophone in five lessons. He is the young man on whom four pair of feminine eyes are fixed in rapt adoration because he surprised the waiter by ordering ham and eggs in French. He is the young man who used to be awkward and ill at ease, but suddenly walks off with the most dazzling girl on the landscape after taking so-and-so's dancing lessons by correspondence. He is the young man with sox appeal and also he is the young man without it.

"He is the model for most of the big collar companies: he is the handsome escort in the ritzy car ads; he's seen everywhere wearing the latest in hats, ties, socks, shoes and what not. And if some day your wife suddenly regards you with disapproval it will be because your noncha-lance with waiters, or your attempted air of careless at-homeness in full dress, doesn't compare favorably with Walter Thornton's."

"Did you say sox appeal?" Adriana asked me. *"Even his feet were perfect for modeling. Look at the sock ads he was in. He was making as much as $200 a week ($3700 according to the 2023 CPI)."* I'll admit, I didn't even know what a "collar ad" was when I first read that passage.

But soon my research revealed the surprising (to me) information that in the 1920s, men's dress shirts and their collars were sold separately. The heavily starched, celluloid collars would be attached to the shirts with two metal collar stays, one in the front, one in the back. The most popular brand of collars at that time was made by the Arrow Collar Company.

The article went on:

"Yet it wasn't so many years ago that this young man was laying bricks. He found, to his own surprise, that he had the perfect, masculine 100-per-cent American features. That includes the ears, too. Few young men have properly pinned on ears, even when the size is all right [...] Mr. Thornton's ears are just right for hats. The hat barely touches the tip, and they are set at a correct angle from the head. Last Easter, he received $50.00 ($900 according to the 2023 CPI) from a well-known hat manufacturer for walking down Fifth Avenue in a high silk hat and being photographed therein."

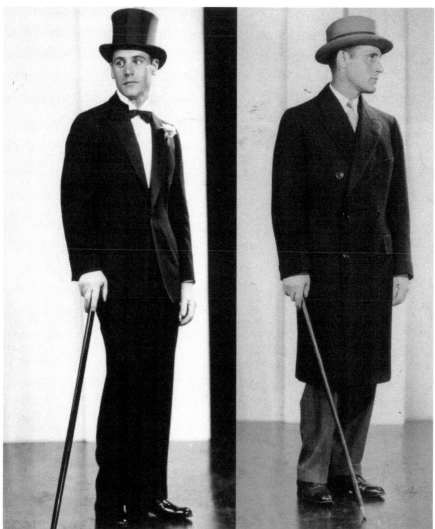

Above: Man in hats. Walter Thornton rather had the men's hat-modeling market cornered during the late 1920s and early 1930s.

"*Famous for his ears! That seems a funny thing to be famous for,*" I'd said at the time.

No one was more surprised by his sudden acclaim as an ideal representation of American youth than Walter himself. "*When I was laying bricks, nobody ever noticed that I was handsome,*" he was quoted as saying in the "Bricklayer" piece. "*It was as much of a surprise to me as anybody.*"

The author of the *New York World* profile continued:

"Mr. Thornton's features, it seems, are so perfect, from the artist's standpoint, that a little can be added here, a bit removed there, say a mustache and a touch of gray at the temples. Thus, the Thornton features have been used as the basis for all six of the men in one advertisement."

Our father attests in the interview to the fact that modeling was not easy. *"Just try to stand balanced on a soap box for half an hour with an ecstatic look in your eyes,"* he said, *"or try to hold a hearty laugh for 25 minutes at a time if you think posing is easy."* He was one of the best-known young men in America! So impressive to know that about our father so early on in his career. This was written nine months after the stock market crash; it talks about his days as a bricklayer but there are no mentions of him going so publicly broke and losing it all.

Walter Thornton modeling/acting shots (Walter Thornton archives)

Chapter 8

I Sell My Own Head

Adriana

A nd now, I turn to the third way that illustrators could work with Walter Thornton and no one else. By 1928 he had a really busy schedule. Commercial picture men used his body for underwear, his form for clothes, his feet for socks, (remember that he even had "sox appeal"!). And, above all, illustrators needed his head, that face, that profile. There was so much demand for him. There simply wasn't enough Walter Thornton to go around!

Perhaps his rapid success as a male model was the thing that had awakened the latent entrepreneur in Walter; it's hard to say, but awaken the entrepreneur it did. The solution to his lack of availability came to Walter in a flash, and it was based on simple mathematics. Good models like him were needed for both illustrations and photographs but, plainly speaking, photographic work paid better. Photographers also worked faster so the models could book multiple assignments for a given day. A male model might earn five dollars an hour for photographic work but just three dollars an hour being drawn by an artist. Walter's idea was simple: create a dummy to go on illustration-posing jobs for him. Drawing on his understanding as a sculptor, he had a plaster cast made of his famous profile and busied himself promoting its sale and rental.

More from the "Bricklayer" (our shorthand name for it) article:

"He presides over a factory which is devoted exclusively to turning out his own head. Already it is sold along with the classic heads and the other regular stock of art dealers. It is, they say, the ideal Twentieth

Century American Type. [...] Now, when an artist calls John Robert Powers of the Actors' and Models' Directory, Mr. Powers can say: 'I'm sorry, Mr. Thornton has a previous engagement today. But I'll be glad to send his head over.'"

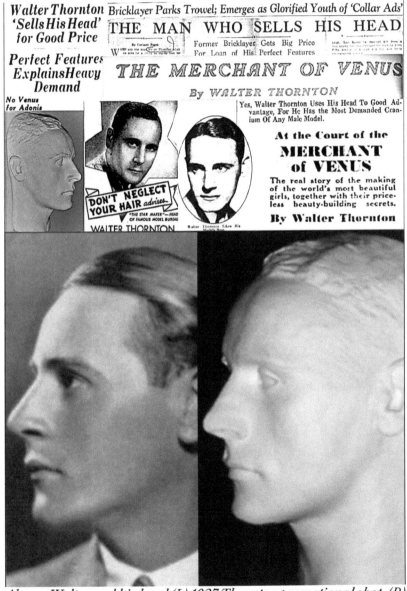

Above: Walter and his head (L) 1927 Thornton promotional shot. (R)
From the Walter Thornton heads, 1928-1931

The "Bricklayer" piece was the first, nationally syndicated article about Walter Thornton we've found. We learned from it that the success of his head business took off from its inception in late 1928. By 1930, more than 3,000 Walter heads had been sold! Our father became known in those circles simply as "The Profile."

When we visited mom's castle in Ajijic, we discovered another mysterious item. It was a wooden shipping crate, about the size (and weight) of a window air conditioner unit. It was so heavy and cumbersome; we had no idea of what to expect. The crate was covered in old postal stickers, proving it had been on a few journeys in its day. As we finally pried the top off the crate, the smell of 'old' told me that the contents hadn't seen the light of day in decades. We still couldn't tell what it was. It was packed in dense wood shavings, that used to be called "excelsior." It appeared to be some kind of statue—something made of plaster. We saw that it contained a reverse-image impression of a life-sized head. Could this be the very mold he used to make his heads?

Yes, we learned, that's exactly what it was. Throughout the many years and many moves, our father must have seen this head mold as sort of a solitary talisman to his past; something he wanted to hang onto (for his family). Though we've still never seen one of the original plaster heads, we found out that they were engraved in the plaster on the bottoms with "Walter Thornton" and one of the years between 1928 and 1931. The inside of the mold was lined with a hardened, waxy, rubber-type material.

We shipped the rest of the contents of Dad's boxes; some to Nancy in Texas and some to me in California, including the crate with the mold, where it sat in my home office for a couple years until I felt compelled to test it, to determine for sure that it was what we thought it was. I bought some plaster of paris, mixed up a batch of it and poured it into the mold. A day later, I removed the hardened impression and inspected it. To my amazement, it appeared to have created an exact duplicate of the Walter Thornton head I'd seen in photographs. I made seven of them, one for each family member. You can imagine what an emotional experience that was for us—to see our father, "The Profile," emerge from the mold, some eighty years later.

We're fortunate to have made those copies when we did, in 2007. In the intervening years, the crate was apparently exposed to heat...and the head melted. Well, the waxy liner did, anyway. There would be no more heads cast from this mold.

In the fall of 1929, with the success and popularity of Walter's Head Factory (that was how he referred to it in interviews), he employed a small crew of assistants, one of whom went on to become a pioneering female illustrator, June Tarpé Mills (1912-1988), who today has a cult of devotees for her proto-feminist, *Marvel* comic strip, "Miss Fury", that she drew under the gender-elusive name, Tarpé Mills.

According to a 1944 article and interview, Mills spoke of working at the head factory as Walter Thornton's assistant while still in her teens, while she also attended art school:

'Thornton had an idea where life-like masks and plaster heads could be used in advertising and thereby, decided to experiment with his own head. Having made casts of plaques and bas-reliefs, I assured him it would be a snap. After generously piling plaster on his head, neck, and shoulders, and testing the plaster's consistency, much as a woman with a broom straw tests a cake, I carefully withdrew the strings which cut the plaster into sections, for easy removal...then waited for the plaster to set---and oboy, did it set! I had pulled the cords too soon and the plaster hardened into one solid mass. Shortly after, Walter was stamping around the studio, desperately clawing at the plaster, which parted reluctantly from his hirsute pate in great chunks. Oddly enough, the mask turned out perfect -- even to being beautifully embellished with most of Walter's eyelashes."

Years later, we would discover a damaged, incomplete copy of the Walter Thornton head company's brochure (Walter Thornton & Co.) from 1929. We now regard it as one of our most treasured relics from our father's early career. The four-page, fold-over brochure featured two close-up photographs of the head, which had been autograph-endorsed by some of the most famous illustrators of the twentieth century

("As fine as the antique classics" – Henry Raleigh; "A good head to have around!" – Chas. Williams).

His 1929 brochure for the heads proclaimed them "good for drawing purposes as well as a decoration." Approximately one-third of the image is ripped away, so we have no idea who else might have endorsed the Walter Thornton heads. But the extant signatures we've been able to decipher provide a stunning cross-section of illustrators. It presents a partial "who's who" of the New York art world of the late 1920s.

Listing of Artists Represented on the 1929 Head

1. J.C. Leyendecker
2. Neysa McMein
3. Henry Raleigh
4. Muriel Dawson
5. H. Weston Taylor
6. McClelland Barclay
7. H. Allen Farnham
8. J. Montgomery Flagg
9. Chas. Williams
10. Howard Chandler Christy
11. Jules Gotlieb
12. W.C. Brigham, Jr.
13. Clayton Knight
14. Will Grefe
15. Reed Crandall
16. George Van Werveke
17. Robert E. MeGinnis
18. Charles D. Mitchell

With in-depth study of the "Bricklayer" article, we were presented with the first timeline conflict that we would run into again and again: trying to prove/disprove the presumed circumstances of the car image. We also found two full-page, full color lithographic ads from the *Saturday Evening Post*, one dated December 1929; and the other one dated March 1930. Both ads were by noted illustrator Percy Edward Anderson, when Walter was perhaps John Robert Powers' most popular male hat model. Those dates seem to show that he survived just fine, continuing to appear in the world's most popular magazines before, directly up to and well after the Crash of '29.

Chapter 9

A New Kid in Town: Enter the Thornton Agency

Nancy

"Managing the World's Most Beautiful Girls"- *Walter Thornton's trademark*

Without question, the most influential eye Walter caught at the beginning of his posing career belonged to John Robert Powers. History has recorded Powers as the man who invented the modeling industry in America, founding his first agency in 1923—though in the beginning, it was not a modeling agency, per se. The ambitious, former stage actor initially formed his agency as a liaison between good-looking, young New York actors and the Broadway stage and silent film industries, in which they were seeking employment.

So in 1926, the Powers Agency's focus was not primarily on models. The agency, still somewhat loosely focused, was financially shored up by its eponymous "charm schools." It eventually would grow into a major beauty conglomerate.

As for representing actors, Powers' focus was centered around the publication of biannual "yearbooks," which contained the photos and basic physical statistics of up-and-coming, would-be film and theater performers (as well as several already-established film and stage stars). It was called the *Actors' Directory & Studio Guide*. John Barrymore and his future wife, Dolores Costello, Billie Dove, Norma Talmadge and

Brian Donlevy were among the notable actors who were also featured alongside Walter Thornton in the January 1927 edition.

Each of the featured actors/subjects was given their own "lookbook" page (photographic catalog with pages of collages that displayed a model's versatility and statistics). The use of catalogs or casting directories representing talent dates back to the early 1900s where new and upcoming actors and actresses would be listed for a chance to get work on the theater stage or in a silent film.

It's crazy to try and imagine it in today's world, but as late as 1929, individual subjects' home telephone numbers were listed in the Powers catalogs, right below their names. That's because each Powers subject was responsible for their own interface with the potential client (though the established film stars were to be contacted through their intermediaries). For instance, if a movie producer was seeking a certain "type," they could refer to the catalogs and contact the individual(s) they were interested in hiring.

After a years-long search of most major online vendors, auction sites and library archives we've never found an extant copy of that Powers catalog. *BUT*, in the craziest of coincidences, the Walter Thornton page is seemingly the only existing page from that January 1927 issue to be found online. It comes via the New York Public Library for the Performing Arts at Lincoln Center. A truly magical find! Thanks, Papi.

WALTER THORNTON
Jerome 6890

Above: Below our dad's name: "Jerome 6 890," using the early twentieth century-style of telephone exchange numbers and letters. Each model would essentially broker their own assignments.

Clients would pay the models through the Powers Agency, which would then take its own five percent cut. Models had latitude in negotiating their own pay rate, too. It would stand to reason that since the Powers Agency was getting a percentage of a given model's ultimate fee, Powers would not have been averse to their models asking for—and receiving—the highest fee they could get. So the Powers Agency was by no stretch of the imagination a one-stop representational hub for models. They didn't book the models' gigs. They didn't negotiate their rates. And they didn't actively scour for their future employment—not in the late 1920s, anyway. On the contrary, most of the talent represented in the book actually paid <u>Powers</u> a monthly retainer fee to remain under his increasingly prestigious banner. His subjects were considered free agents. As such, they were not exclusive to the Powers Agency. There wouldn't have been any reason to make any of them exclusive—since there was no competition...until the Walter Thornton Model Agency opened in 1930. It was fascinating to go back in time and learn about the founding of a specific type of agency that had never existed before and to learn it through the life of the very man who conceived it...our dad.

Walter was a keen observer; he had to be, to survive on the streets as a child. He was a fast learner, and his amiable nature helped him make contacts in the world of art and theater. Early on he worked when he could, posing at night while making films during his day job. But as his looks grew in popularity, he would concentrate solely on modeling. He now had a bird's-eye view to watch his employers and colleagues. He was eager to understand their needs and further succeed in his work. Then one afternoon he took a break from posing and noticed illustrator Arthur William Brown—later famous for his work in the *Saturday Evening Post*—making call after call and growing more agitated with each unsuccessful conversation.

Brown was seeking a model with particular attributes, but making the connection wasn't simple at the time. Most models didn't have representation at all and promoted themselves individually to artists, who turned to their address books and notes—and memory—when a need arose. This led to a rather inefficient system, where the lack of a centralized schedule wasted artists' and models' time and made it doubly difficult for employers to find the perfect fit for a shoot. When a rush job arose, advertisers and artists would mostly be obliged to accept their third or fourth choice.

Walter gave the problem some thought. As an established model himself, he understood the needs of both parties and had the industry contacts to connect the two. Why not begin a new kind of agency, he thought, one that would specifically represent models only? One that took a much more active role in exchange for its fee. Why not centralize the promotion and booking of models, similar to the way employment agencies operated?

The Walter Thornton Model Agency was, in fact, the very *first* agency in America designed specifically to represent photographic advertisement models, an uncharted territory in the early 1930s. He called it "an employment agency for models." The WTMA was indeed something altogether new and different. The stacks of articles and library references we uncovered online described, at great length, how our father didn't just found a modeling agency—he was instrumental in founding the entire modeling, beauty and advertising industries in America. The basic industry template struck by the Walter Thornton Model Agency became one that is mainly adhered to by major modeling agencies to this very day.

And the press generated by the start of his new agency was of the level that any other new business could normally only dream of. We found this glowing piece from a 1931 *New York Daily Mirror*, written by columnist Jack Lait—a Broadway-beat writer. Excerpts from the article are transcribed below.

Highlights of Broadway
From the Circle to the Square
by JACK LAIT

Peddles Pulchritude

SIX years ago he was a bricklayer. Today he has hundreds of the most beautiful girls in the land at his beck and call. Literally. And I don't mean just pretty girls. I mean the ones who flash the teeth and dimples at you from magazine covers and high-priced ads, many of whom have been glorified by Ziegfeld, vaniteered by Carroll and scandalized by White. He has a big model bureau patronized by many of New York's foremost photographers, advertising agencies and artists. His name is Walter Thornton.

Thornton, himself the most sought-after male model in America, has virtually retired from posing to devote himself to his business. He was the Dobbs hat fellow, whose face was almost as familiar as Washington's on postage stamps. Georgia Warren, painter of men, discovered him—on a bench in the park—in the romantic manner; she strained her eyes: Those ears! That neck! That profile! Those shoulders! She walked over and asked him if he'd pose. He thought she was crazy. But she convinced him there was money in it. And he wasn't crazy.

Soon he was posing for J. C. Leyendecker, Neysa McMein, John La Gatta, Bradshaw Crandall, McClelland Barclay, C. D. Williams, Saul Tepper, and no end of advertisers. James Montgomery Flagg, Norman Rockwell and Howard Chandler Christy used his head. Commercial picture men used his body for underwear, his form for clothes, his feet for sox—he had even sox appeal. There was so much demand for Thornton's head that he had a mold struck off and made plaster

casts which he sold or rented out, being the world's only multiple model. He now sells them at so much a head and has disposed of more than 3,000. He met other models and, in helping them, he eased himself into model-procuring and supplying as a profession.

Now, on his lists are countless raving beauties in variety to fill any need—any size hand, foot, waist, calf; any height, any weight, any complexion, any age, any type. Some of them earn $150 a week. They pay him 10 per cent. They are from all walks of life, including big-shot society. Claire Cole is Mrs. Schuyler Lott, Jr., Virginia Randall is the daughter of the master of the Leviathan.

I've known Walter a long time. I sat talking with him the other day in his swanky office. He was toying with one of the plaster casts of his head, which he had sent in for to give me as a souvenir. He tossed it up and caught it and twirled it without even looking at it. There was something so natural about the way he did it, something so familiar—suddenly it flashed on me:

Did you ever watch a bricklayer handle a brick?

Walter Thornton, Model Gent and Model
'gent—Once a Bricklayer—
Never Again.

Above: New York Daily Mirror, October 27, 1931 Albuquerque Journal
(Albuquerque, New Mexico) October 4, 1931, page 10

Highlights of Broadway From the Circle to the Square By Jack Lait

"Six years ago he was a bricklayer. Today he has hundreds of the most beautiful girls in the land at his beck and call. Literally. And I don't mean just pretty girls. I mean the ones who flash the teeth and dimples at you from magazine covers and high-priced ads, many of whom have been glorified by Ziegfeld, vaniteered by Carroll and scandalized by White. He has a big model bureau patronized by many of New York's foremost photographers, advertising agencies and artists. His name is Walter Thornton. Thornton, himself the most sought-after male model in America, has virtually retired from posing to devote himself to his business. He was the Dobbs hat fellow, whose face was almost as familiar as Washington's on postage stamps. He met other models and, in helping them, he eased himself into model-procuring and supplying as a profession. Now, on his lists are countless raving beauties in variety to fill any need—any size hand, foot, waist, calf; any height, any weight, any complexion, any age, any type. Some of them earn $150 a week. They pay him 10 per cent. They are from all walks of life, including big-shot society. Claire Cole is Mrs. Schuyler Lott, Jr. Virginia Randall is the daughter of the master of the Leviathan.

"I've known Walter for a long time. I sat talking with him the other day in his swanky office. He was toying with one of the plaster casts of his head, which he had sent in to give me as a souvenir. He tossed it up and caught it and twirled it without even looking at it. There was something so natural about the way he did it, something so familiar-suddenly it flashed on me: Did you ever watch a bricklayer handle a brick?"

From our dad's boxes, we pulled out a first edition copy of Dale Carnegie's *How to Win Friends and Influence People*. Dad seemed to have a Dale Carnegie quote for just about every occasion.

The book contained short, common-sense aphorisms that offered positive advice. We'd vaguely guessed he might have been a friend of our father from his New York life; a friend who sure liked to hand out advice. When I opened the well-thumbed, hardcover edition of the Dale Carnegie book, a newspaper clipping fluttered to the floor. It had turned a sepia tone through the years. The article was written by Dale Carnegie himself. And it was all about Walter Thornton. The entire article. From his December 26, 1940, nationally syndicated newspaper column, "Dale Carnegie: Author *of How To Win Friends and Influence People*":

DALE CARNEGIE
Author of 'How to Win Friends and Influence People'

IF YOU had gone to Chillicothe, O., a few years ago you might have seen a tallish boy driving a delivery wagon for a butcher. If you had made inquiry, you would have found that he was an orphan who had to earn his own living.

Not much chance for an orphan driving a butcher wagon, is there?

But this orphan, Walter Thornton, who saved up his money chauffering the butcher wagon, came to New York where he tried to get work. Having no special training, he found it pretty hard to shake salt on the tail of a job. But at last he got one in the shipping department of a film agency; all day, he crated film and sent it to the theaters; uncrated it when it got back.

Mr. Carnegie

'If you had gone to Chillicothe, O. a few years ago you might have seen a tallish boy driving a delivery wagon for a butcher. If you had made inquiry, you would have found that he was an orphan who had to earn his own living. Not much chance for an orphan driving a butcher wagon, is there? But this orphan, Walter Thornton, who saved his money chauffeuring the butcher wagon, came to New York, where he tried to get work [...]. He heard there were good paying jobs posing as artists' models. He had a good build, was fairly good looking; so he decided to try for such a job [...]. Couldn't he establish some kind of agency for handling models for artists? A sort of employment agency? When he told his friends he had an idea for starting an employment agency for models, they laughed at him. Said also that he had no business experience. True. But he had something more valuable: An idea, and the determination to go ahead.

He established his own agency; and now has the biggest business of its kind in the world. And he has done this in ten years.

Why has Walter Thornton succeeded? Chiefly because he originated a new idea; something no one had thought of before. And stuck to it till he put it over. Simple."

"You've got to read this right now. It seems pretty significant to me," I excitedly told Adriana.

"Wow...he speaks of our dad so...heroically!" she said after reading it.

"I know," I replied. *"It paints him as a total success story—starting a new industry!"*

We later learned that Dale Carnegie's very first successful book was called *Public Speaking: A Practical Course for Business Men* (1926), the year after he and Walter had first crossed paths and eleven years before *How to Win Friends and Influence People* became a phenomenon. In the eighty-five-plus years since the latter book's first publication, it is estimated to have sold over thirty million copies, in just about every language on the planet. In 2020, the New York Public Library ranked Carnegie's *How to Win Friends and Influence People* as the sixth most checked-out book in the NYPL's one hundred twenty-five-year history.

Of course, nothing could ever be all roses and sunshine. The tabloid gossip columnists were always trying to fuel a supposed blood rivalry between Powers and Thornton, though we've never found any evidence to suggest that John Robert Powers and Walter Thornton were anything but friendly, gentlemanly rivals—a little surprising, in light of the fact that our father essentially decamped from the Powers Agency to become the closest thing to what JRP had as a competitor. Powers even continued representing Walter Thornton for limited modeling jobs until at least 1931—over a year after our father started his own agency. We think that fact stands as proof that their parting was an amicable one. There seemed to be no rancor over the fact that some of Walter's former colleagues at the Powers Agency also modeled under the Thornton Agency flag (Brian Donlevy and Neil Hamilton are examples), soon after it opened.

But there was nothing made-up about the long-time rivalry between Walter Thornton and Harry Conover. The Harry Conover Agency opened its doors in 1939 and eventually became the third prong of the triumvirate known as "The Big Three" of the New York/Hollywood modeling agents, as they were called in a lengthy profile article in *LIFE Magazine* in 1945. Conover himself was another former J.R. Powers model-turned-agent. Once the erratic newcomer made his way into the model-booking game, his first piece of nasty gamesmanship was by promising the sun, moon and everything in between to one of the Thornton Agency's up-and-coming models, one Anita Counihan. Walter had her so busy posing that she was earning over a hundred dollars a week ($2027 according to the 2023 CPI).

Conover changed her name to Anita "The Face" Colby. That was how she was billed. She is referred to today as "America's First Supermodel." The Anita Colby caper was not an isolated incident. One of the ways that Conover built his roster was to hang out on the sidewalk outside the Thornton Agency and intercept departing girls, models that Walter had groomed and trained and spent time and money bringing along. Conover would then promise them more money modeling for him! Walter's dislike of Conover was sincere, to be sure. Conover was a piece of work, a schemer and a model-poacher by all accounts. Even his own daughter, Carole Conover, didn't have good things to say about him in a book she wrote. Walter saw straight through him and made every effort to avoid any dealings with him whenever possible.

The official chronicle of the earliest days of the professional modeling business—especially the male modeling business—has yet to be comprehensively told. As such, piecing together this largely undocumented subject of those years has been a challenge. Learning that our father was actually a beauty industry pioneer immediately following the stock market crash of 1929 was pretty thrilling to contemplate. What's more, the Walter Thornton Model Agency is on a very short list of successful and prominent American companies to have launched in the months surrounding the crash.

Chapter 10

The Model King

Adriana

T he Walter Thornton Model Agency opened its very first office in the iconic Chrysler Building, becoming one of that building's very first tenants. *"Can you believe Dad made the newspaper as a tenant of the Chrysler building?"* Nancy said. Of all the other hundreds of tenants, we were very fortunate to find his name listed in the Real Estate Transactions section of the New York Herald Tribune of 1930 next to other two other tenants of large national firms.

Working in the New York modeling world since 1925, Walter had many connections within the advertising industries of fashion and beauty. He started small, representing hand-picked favorites that he'd worked with before. He slowly added to his roster, eventually representing literally thousands of models, spread over a twenty-five-year period.

He seems to have preferred unknown models that he could mold into the Walter Thornton look and style of the early 1930s. He would represent male, female and child models, as well. Any attractive person could be a model. Even housewives. Even policemen. As his eventual beauty conglomerate grew, the agency's name morphed into the more all-encompassing Walter Thornton, Inc.

Taking a cue from Powers and other theatrical casting services, Walter improved upon the idea and published his own agency "lookbook" that was dispersed to advertising agencies, corporate clients, photographers, artists, publications and illustrators. Lookbook is still a term that is very much used in the modeling and fashion industries of today. In our father's boxes, we found loose pages from his lookbooks or catalogs from the early 1930s. Some models posed in plain clothes, some in evening dresses, some in equestrian clothing and some in lingerie.

"*Look at our dad's beautiful models from the 1930s with measurements and all! This is history! We need to record all of this,*" Nancy said. Looking at the lingerie photos, we realized that whatever was popular back then is still popular now.

"*I just saw a Facebook advertisement for a body shaper just like this!*" I noted. "*Clothing styles have changed throughout the years but not the body shapers.*" We both laughed.

During late 1931, word of Walter Thornton's catalog reached the ears of Louis Sobol. The Broadway columnist who was always on the lookout for the new and exciting, filed the following report. "There's a concern in town," Sobol wrote in his "Voice of Broadway" column, "which publishes a tome containing the pictures of all the city's beauties—detailing all dimensions, color of hair, size of calves and phone numbers. ... Don't jump to conclusions—it's for artists and advertising agencies who want models."

Above: Page from Walter Thornton Inc. lookbook 1931

In the first few years, Walter's modeling agency wasn't the only part of his life that was flourishing. His personal life was also given quite a boost when one of his models, Judy Dolan, became Mrs. Walter Thornton in 1934! And despite the societal expectations of that era, she was a working wife. She would be an invaluable help in the business, ultimately managing the men's division.

What set our dad's agency apart as a first was, of course, his specialization. Stepping away from Powers' catchall approach of talent representation, Walter created a bureau for models only. Walter actually discouraged hiring actors and actresses, as they were more invested in their acting careers than modeling. But he found out, all too often, that once he invested time and money into the grooming, training and promotion of a model, they often were lured to Hollywood. In a revealing 1934 interview, both Walter and his new wife, Judy, spoke to their frustration that resulted from their 'success stories'—the models who had left to make it big on the silver screen. "*We have financed hundreds and hundreds of girls,*" Judy said, "*and only about a dozen have ever paid us back.*" Some of Mrs. Thornton's support even included lending the girls her personal wardrobe. Likewise, Walter would regularly lose some of his top female models to society marriages with moneyed bachelors who would woo his models into matrimony and early retirement from the modeling business. Remember, unlike Mrs. Thornton, this was an era where it was okay for young women to work before marriage but certainly *not after*. And, make no mistake, Walter Thornton models were being considered ideal "trophy brides".

At some later point in time, our dad seemed to have made an uneasy peace with this "occupational hazard" in running a modeling agency: Beauty was what made the Hollywood world go 'round. So, if it was inevitable that he was going to lose people to Tinseltown careers, there was nothing that said he couldn't capitalize on it by promoting the Walter Thornton Model Agency as the "discoverer" of said star. After all, he had picked her from many hopefuls and invested a considerable amount of time and money on training (developing) the person. The best way to protect his investment, of course, had to be with a penalty clause for early withdrawal from their contracts, which was a financially steep one. After all, business was business, and this Merchant was not giving any Venuses away for free. But he was fair, not extortionate, when settling with models who decided to break their contracts with his agency.

His resolve was tested with Lucille Wilds, one of his top models in the late 1930s. Lucille, known for her toothpaste-ad smile, began working for the Thornton agency in 1937, while she was still a minor. Her mother had happily signed the contract and ten-thousand-dollar marriage penalty clause (as a matter of fact, she had insisted on that particular clause), being that she was ambitious for her daughter's career, and concerned that marriage might bring it to an early end. Lucille, in turn, had ratified the agreement when she came of age extending the contract four more years. But by 1939, she had fallen in love with a fellow model and changed her mind. She wanted to get married...without delay. Lucille asked Walter to release her from the contract. Thornton said no. He was only starting to realize a return on the two-and-a-half-years of investment he had put into making her over and building her career with constant promotion. A 1938 *Look Magazine* article, featuring Wilds, stated that she spent $1560 per year on clothes ($33,000 according to the 2023 CPI) and Walter was footing most of that. So, Lucille hired an attorney and went on a public strike, barricading herself in her hotel room and refusing to work. Calls came in fast and furious from ad agencies wanting to feature this romantic heroine in their campaigns. Newspapers took sides. Lucille's mother was on Thornton's side; Lucille's father supported his daughter. Judy Thornton was on the side of romance and walked out of the Thornton home, refusing to return with their daughter, Daryl, until her agent husband let the young couple wed.

Finally, a few weeks after the news broke, Walter tore up the contract, acknowledging they were now free to marry without penalty. He had one condition: that Lucille continue modeling for him for "at least six months." A thankful Lucille Wilds went one better. The following year, she participated in and was named "Dream Girl of 1940" in a contest judged by artists, photographers, and art directors in Atlantic City. In fact, Lucille Wilds did continue modeling for the Walter Thornton Agency for some time. We later made contact with her son Lance Lee who wrote a book about his family. It was interesting to learn that Lucille Wilds, who ended up not marrying her fellow model, married David Levy, the creator of *The Addams Family* television series (1964-1966) based on the original Charles Addams New Yorker cartoons.

T he improved, full-service operation that Walter Thornton formulated for his agency made him feel justified in doubling John Robert Powers Agency standard cut of five percent of all models' earnings—Walter was *a ten-percenter.*

Our dad developed a complete hands-on management approach for his agency. As he described in later newspaper and magazine interviews, his idea was to groom a smaller, more select stable of models, for whom he would provide everything the model might need, such as physical improvement regimens, guidance, handholding, lessons in poise and posture, and stylistic makeovers, with each model receiving their weekly bookings every Monday morning at the Chrysler Building. "No experience" was fine by him. His would be an exclusive roster of perfectly groomed, always professional, reliable models; the epitome of the wholesome, American beauty. The languid, sexualized models and actresses who followed the Ziegfeld Follies template of beauty—"The Long-Stemmed American Beauty Roses," as Ziegfeld called them—were not in the plan for Walter's outfit.

Above: Models getting their assignments from Walter Thornton, 1935.

Powers continued to promote the same female beauty ideal that Ziegfeld had (tall, lanky, willowy), about 5' 9", and measuring 34-24-34. His high-fashion models adhered to the motto, "Slender, Tender." Walter seemed to sense that styles had shifted in the years that followed the Wall Street Crash. Especially in product advertisements. Women wanted relatable models; models who were more like them. With the Depression going on, female consumers would not have been likely to connect with a leggy vixen, draped on a satin lounge, selling them Malt-O-Meal.

The Walter Thornton Agency opted for more natural, slightly curvier models. The average measurements of his petite models who were most popular with photographers and advertising men were 5' 5" tall, weighed one 112 pounds, and measured 34-25-36. His high fashion models' average height was 5' 7", weighing 118 pounds, with 34-25-34 measurements. We must note that model measurements evolved with the times like everything else, but we were proud to find out that. Our father was perhaps the first in the industry to advocate for, and promote, better health standards in the modeling field. It worried him to see so many models dieting themselves into hospitals, sanitariums, and sometimes premature deaths just trying to maintain that perfect size.

Not only did he publicly advise his models to eat more to keep their curves, but once he signed a model, she was required to retain her minimum proportions and weight as shown in her original registration card. That is, they could gain but not lose weight (within reason). To enforce his rule, the models were weighed and measured regularly. If they appeared ill from self- imposed famine diets and looked like they were losing weight too fast, they would be sent home to recuperate under a doctor's care and would not be booked out on modeling jobs again until they were healthy. And his effort to work with healthy girls was one that he maintained throughout his years as an agent from the 1930s to the 1950s.

His great specialty was the sometimes total remaking of a given model's appearance. In later interviews he said that he always took it as a personal challenge to be able to detect and smooth down a model's rough edges and give them the style and confidence needed for success as a Walter Thornton model. He was regularly featured in the press as "Beauty Expert Walter Thornton", beginning as early as 1931.

One of my personal favorites is the 1931 interview that dubbed him, "The Master of Callaesthetics." I sure had to get out the *Cassell's Spanish/English, English/Spanish Dictionary* for that one. Loosely defined, it means the very theory of beauty; a system of principles for the appreciation of beauty and aesthetics. Apparently, it was not as snappy a title as "The Merchant of Venus," since it never caught on. Thank heavens.

His experiences as an actor and model had prepared him to become the spokesman for this world of glamour and beauty. Proper diet. Skin care. Fashion. Exercise regimens. He seemed to be the undisputed authority when it came to every aspect of beauty.

Our dad described in an early interview how, during his modeling years, he wasn't just mindlessly staring into the distance whilst he was posing. He was staring into his future, formulating his escape plan. Modeling, for him, was just a stepping stone, and he was dreaming of greater challenges than merely standing, stock-still, maintaining an expressionless mask for the rest of his life. Besides, he knew that models usually had fairly short careers (though men could work for longer). Once the novelty of his new position wore off and the stultifying boredom set in, the very act of modeling itself became tiresome. *"Looking relaxed can be exhausting,"* I remember my dad once saying, though I can't recall in what context.

Since the earliest days of advertisement modeling, the models were mostly beautiful young subjects. But in another innovation, the Walter Thornton Agency also had a stable of "character" models: the impish child with freckles and prominently missing teeth; the matronly society woman; the stately, middle-aged banker-type. The agency aimed to be a one-stop modeling hub. And if there was a very specific request for, say, red-headed triplets, if they didn't have any on hand, they were connected enough to be able to find them.

Our half-sister Daryl (born in 1935 to Walter and Judy) began her own posing career before her first birthday, and quite by accident. The agency had arranged for a diaper ad job requiring five baby models, already somewhat of a juggling act if the client expected all five infants to be happy, charming and in the mood to be photographed at the same time. Then one of the infants became ill. At the client's insistence, Walter frantically cast about for a suitable fill-in, and finding none, rang his wife. That was Daryl's first modeling gig, and she continued in the business for years. *"I envy her bank account,"* Walter said in a 1937 interview, *"because it is strictly one way—in."*

Even after going through every file in our father's papers, we never did come across any kind of manifest or log of every single model our father represented. This made it even more difficult to pinpoint exactly who got their modeling starts with the Walter Thornton Model Agency, since many of them modeled under different names and in some cases, multiple names. Eventually, the running of the male model division got handed over to Dad's first wife, Judy, and we've been able to confirm some of the men the Thornton Agency employed before they went on to Hollywood stardom. In addition to Brian Donlevy (*Beau Geste*),

Alan Curtis (*High Sierra*), Neil Hamilton (*Commissioner Gordon* in the *Batman* TV series), and Robert Kent (*The Phantom Rider*, modeled under the name Douglas Blackley, Jr.), there was also Bob Hutton, who during WWII was seen as a "second-string Jimmy Stewart," when Stewart went off to war. There was also a handsome, blonde ex-GI named Bill Williams, who would star opposite Susan Hayward in a 1946, film noir classic called *Deadline at Dawn* (a feature film with two Thornton alumni co-stars!).

Watching television with our father was always entertaining. His accompanying monologues were much more interesting and certainly funnier than whatever was playing on one of the two stations with sporadic antenna reception. Many times, especially when watching old Hollywood movies and black-and-white television shows, he seemed to have an unusually familiar knowledge about the actors and actresses who appeared on screen. American, English-language films were not commonly shown on the Ajijic TV stations when we were kids. But when we would happen upon a Hollywood movie, our father would give a regular running commentary. He sometimes mentioned the actors as "*someone I used to know*," or "*someone I met once*." We grew up with this vague notion that our dad somehow knew, or at least had met everyone who appeared in old, English-language films or TV shows—especially the black and white ones.

Above: (L to R) Joseph Cotten (Wikipedia), Neil Hamilton with a dog (Walter Thornton archive) Below: (L to R) Ruth Starrett and Robert Kent (Walter Thornton lookbook page), Brian Donlevy (Walter Thornton archive)

"*I used to know that guy, Joe Cotten*," our dad once casually mentioned, when the actor appeared in a detective movie we happened upon. "*I knew him when we were very young.*"Joseph Cotten, we would learn, was one of the Walter Thornton Model Agency's very first male models in the beginning of the 1930s. All the while that he modeled for our dad, he continued trying his hand at acting. It was his association with Orson Welles, which began in 1934, that would change everything for him. Cotten went on to become one of Hollywood's top leading men of the 1940s and 50s, though at the start of the Depression, he relied upon his handsome face, his former-lifeguard physique, and our dad's guidance, to get by in the post-crash years.

O ur one goal and our initial research had been to simply find out what the story was behind the *Seabiscuit* photo. To that end, we tried to stay focused on the years surrounding the stock market crash, from roughly 1928 to 1930 in order to find out how he had so drastically misplayed the Wall Street stock market, among other things. But in pretty short order, it was looking less and less possible that he had 'lost all'. Evidence just kept mounting to the contrary.

At the time of the crash Walter was living in a small, walkup flat on MacDougal Street in Greenwich Village. But with his new agency seeing rapid success, he soon moved uptown to the luxurious Mayflower Hotel, at Columbus Circle in late 1930. We'd never known our father to be much of a great financial risk-taker—and we had surely never known him to be any kind of gambling daredevil. We couldn't imagine why he would have risked everything he had, speculating on a crazily volatile stock market, and at such a pivotal time in his career. From "bankrupt investor" to "The Model King' in just over a year's time? At the very least, wouldn't that have been considered one of the great comebacks of the twentieth century? Almost like Seabiscuit, himself.

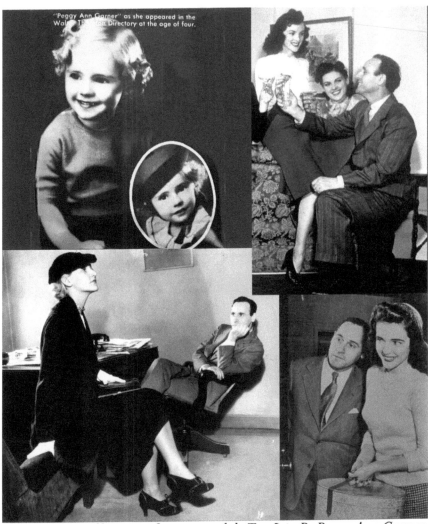

Above: Some of his most famous models Top L to R: Peggy Ann Garner, Peggy Diggins. Bottom L to R: Dolores Donlon, and Cathy Downs (Walter Thornton archive)

Chapter 11

The World's Toughest Job

Nancy

It is a glamorous, interesting calling, yes, but WHAT A LIFE! -Walter Thornton

As we sifted through a multitude of photographs featuring our father in his office, a pattern emerged. Typically these pictures showcased him surrounded by a bevy of stunning women. These images kindled our curiosity, prompting us to delve deeper into the inner workings of Dad's profession. How did he establish the first photographic advertising modeling agency, crafting an organizational framework to manage his models? His journey lacked a precedent to emulate.

We wondered about the process a model went through to become a Venus for The Merchant. With no clear guidelines for him to follow, the path remained enigmatic. Did it involve a linear A-to-Z sequence, or was it more intuitive? Walter Thornton mentioned in an Associated Press article that he constantly heard from men expressing astonishment that he enjoyed the company of beautiful women daily, all while receiving compensation. These sentiments echoed the public's perception, who thought of his role as effortless and glamorous.

However, Walter was swift to dispel this notion, asserting that the facade presented to the public concealed a range of headaches and demanding work. Beyond the surface charm lay a world replete with challenges, unveiling a combination between perception and reality that only those within the industry truly comprehend. In his words: *"managing the world's most beautiful girls is the world's toughest job."*

Above: Walter Thornton working with his models including Susan Hayward. cira. 1938 (Walter Thornton archive)

So how did it all work? Methodically. He had a very clear and detailed operational system. Despite the fact that each week hundreds of girls would just show up as unscheduled walk-ins, Thornton did not encourage personal visits until an appointment was made. That was the first step of his process. In hoping to obtain this appointment, the prospective model would send in a snapshot (no professional picture) together with information of their personal statistics (age, height, weight, hair color, eye color, measurements, dress size, shoe size) and a telephone number.

If Thornton was impressed by the subject's beauty in the photograph, or if he thought that they would make a good "type" or "character" he would instruct one of his office people to arrange an appointment for the lucky applicant. A female interviewer would receive her (or him, as the case may have been). The model-to-be would be asked numerous screening questions such as "why?" and "full-time job or part-time job?" "prior experience?" "willingness to learn?" "level of education?" among others.

The best candidates would then be passed through to meet Walter personally. He certainly had personal preferences, calling the ideal girl one "whose form reflects the appealing qualities of vigor, strength and health," but he always stopped short of declaring a beauty standard. Each model hopeful, Walter said, must be imagined "through a thousand eyes"—the eyes of potential clients. Walter could not describe the ideal woman because to him, beauty was exclusively in the eye of the beholder.

Conversely, some candidates weren't hired for their beauty at all. Because even if you were not particularly beautiful, you might have shapely and graceful legs that would be useful in stocking, shoe or lingerie ads. Or you might have beautiful hands, with tapered fingers for jewelry and nail-polish ads.

By the early 1930s, four main types had been identified by the agency, though variation could and did happen. Walter described the types this way: "*One is the ingenue or juvenile who is, or looks, eighteen. She has an appealing smile, wide lustrous eyes and a natural vivacity and sweetness. Second is the college type ... a wholesome, outdoor girl, well-built, athletic, intelligent. The kind of girl who walks in the rain and through the autumn leaves in tailored tweed clothes. The next is the sophisticate—sleekly groomed, poised and a bit haughty. Often she is exotic and languorous.*"

The last, and best, type would be something of an all-arounder. This girl possessed the flexibility to be perceived as many different types from pretty springtime bride, to the housewife that suffers all those terrible aches and pains, to a glamorous cover girl. This was the girl you might not even take notice of, so casual, normal and natural was her appeal. But with her adaptable smile, change of hairstyle, wardrobe and makeup, and her ability to project her imagination, she could make you believe she was all of the above and more, too.

Once those factors were sorted, the new recruit went through the same tried-and-true process every other Thornton Agency model did. There'd be make-up and hair-styling lessons, skincare tips, and directions on how to walk and pose. Color schemes, wardrobe planning and figure control. And, of course, the proper way to speak to clients, illustrators and photographers. All of this "how-to" learning would be widely adapted in later years as curriculum for the Walter Thornton Model and Charm Schools across the U.S. and Canada.

Physical perfection wasn't all of it. The girl had to have that ineffable "it." Walter defined "it" as *one third poise, one third intelligence, and one third sex appeal.* This commodity could be categorized. A girl who had "it" for hair and face—regardless of her other attributes—might be a photographer's dream on a hair products shoot. A girl with "it" for ankles and feet could model shoes, and the photographer wouldn't give one whit whether there was a model nearby with a prettier face.

Even the most gorgeous models couldn't hope for much success if they were not intelligent enough or their personality prevented them from being able to act. A model needed to register emotions on cue and convey a story through her face, body, hands, and especially her smile. *"Learn to make your smile talk,"* he advised young model hopefuls. The mood she projected had to be spontaneous, genuine and convincing, even while maintaining the same pose for extended periods of time. Ad campaigns and magazine illustrations told a story that models had to convey, and the client needed to feel confident that their subject would deliver. Walter was exacting with his requirements, knowing that despite the apparent glamor of the model's lifestyle, it was a job.

There was another chief requirement that had nothing to do with physical attributes or performing abilities. It was the all-important need for punctuality, and it was something that could never be violated. The new recruits would be taught the idea that "if you're on time, you're late" was the way to operate. It was this commitment to punctuality that Walter himself had always used when he modeled, and it was this professional behavior that made him even more popular.

Once Walter sensed she was ready, the girl was then launched. And what were the chances, the odds, of even making it to the launching pad? Pretty damn slim. Of all those people that crossed the threshold of the agency, one out of every one thousand made it. And only one out of every five thousand made it to the top.

The most exacting and nerve-wracking part of the whole journey was the launch, Walter said, because so much of a model's hopes for success came down to precisely *how* he presented her to his clients. One slipup could ruin all of it. For the launch, the girl had to be photographed extensively according to her type. This called for more than one photo shoot with more than one photographer. After the sessions, the negatives of the best photographs would be grouped together and developed onto a composite or montage page with the detailed measurements of the candidate and any of the special attributes of the model such as lovely hands, blond hair, perfect smile, or exceptional profile. This would become the girl's personal page in the agency catalog. These photo composites had to showcase the girl with the perfect hairstyle for each outfit and had to be in the appropriate mood and pose.

All these factors, and dozens of others, were considered just to present a cohesive representation of this girl in such a way that would make a client stop from turning to the next page of the catalog. Then hundreds of copies of her catalog page were made. And just how did these newly minted models get placement into the Walter Thornton Model Agency catalogs? On a regularly scheduled basis, the agency's Traffic Manager would get a handful of the latest models' pages to office messengers who would make the rounds of the hundreds of clients locally (and by mail for faraway accounts) and place the new pages in the catalogs (loose-leaf binders, actually). They would also remove the pages of any models who were no longer available to work. After that, calls were made, appointments were made, girls picked up their assignment slips from the agency's office, photo shoots happened, ads were composed, and the reading public had an unending parade of beauty marching through their favorite magazines.

It sounded like a lot, but in reality, the launch was merely the first step in a model's career. A beautiful model was nothing without visibility; she needed to be noticed in order to be called in for a job. And Walter's role was to make sure his models were noticed by the right people.

LIFE Magazine called him "an energetic agent with a keen publicist's eye," and, in the advertising world, it was the publicists who decided and directed cultural trends. A virtual "parade of models" (which irked *Mrs.* Thornton to no end) accompanied the Thorntons to parties and moved through their lives and social circle, gaining the exposure that would result in modeling jobs.

Being seen with wealthy socialites could easily turn into lucrative contracts for some girls when their celebrity-by-proxy made them advertising gold. But only a fraction of his girls were celebrity enough to appear at the Stork Club and get mentioned in the gossip pages, so Walter searched for creative ways to showcase the other women he represented. He printed calendars featuring his most popular models and sent them to local celebrities, columnists and other media influencers.

From the earliest days of the agency, he partnered with beauty columnists like Delight Dixon, supplying his models to illustrate beauty tips and tricks—on condition that they be listed as Thornton models. Some of his models endorsed products by virtue of their celebrity. And for his own part, Walter endorsed men's products ranging from hair cream to razors, always on the strength of his role as a model manager rather than as a model himself. Sometimes his female models played a role in his ads, too.

Above: Walter modeling

Walter even published his own content creation, running a newspaper series called "American Beauties" that profiled models he wanted to introduce or promote. A more extensive, photo-heavy series, "At the Court of the Merchant of Venus" ran later, boasting "candid" and posed photos, giving the reader a chance to get to know the girls behind the advertisements. Usually, these pieces contained beauty advice from the model herself, encouraging the reader to make the most of her own features. And always, the model's credibility was summarized in four key words: "A Walter Thornton model." Later, when the agency became known for the pinup girl, he changed his branding to match: "A Walter Thornton pinup."

These promotional ventures had the same, single aim: putting the right model in the right place at the right time to get her noticed and get her work. But every once in a while, Walter would reverse the tactic on this publicity strategy if he thought it best for a particular model's career. In those cases he would flood the market with a new face, then hide her from the world—and from talent scouts—for as long as a few months. This was a risky and costly choice, but with the right model, it paid off when, because of her sudden invisibility, producers or ad men grew desperate to sign her. In the right situation, a young model could make ten times what she might have earned had she modeled steadily throughout.

Of course, despite his best-laid plans, his system of operation didn't always play out as smoothly as it was supposed to. With two hundred models in the agency's roster there were bound to be issues in the office to deal with.

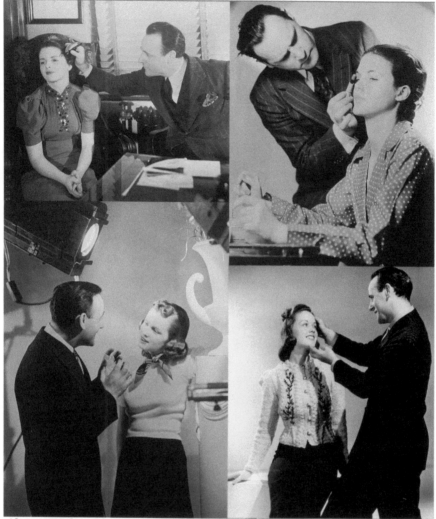

Above: Walter Thornton working with his models circa. 1931- 934 (Walter Thornton archive)

Occasionally, certain models embarked on ventures both unforeseen and astonishing. An instance arose where a valued client, faced with an impending project, contacted Thornton's office to secure the services of a specific brunette model with whom they had previously collaborated on a significant assignment. To the agency's dismay, the following day brought a call from the client who was angry and confused. Instead of the brunette they had urgently sought, a blonde model had been dispatched by the agency.

It turned out that the brunette model had undertaken an impromptu transformation, bleaching her hair overnight. Amidst the client's justified ire, a ripple effect was set into motion. The model's meticulously crafted marketing profile and agency catalog page, which had been produced with considerable effort and expense, was now obsolete.

While some models excelled during training, they found themselves immobilized in the presence of a client's camera on an actual assignment. Among them was a girl whose captivating smile held an undeniable charm but who faltered when asked to embody different emotions. Her ability to convey anything beyond that signature smile seemed to be an elusive feat.

Regrettably, she remained incapable of registering alternate sentiments, regardless of the scenario presented. Walter, wanting an expression of fear and urgency, painted a vivid picture of a car hurtling towards her. "*Imagine the imminent collision*," he implored, hoping to draw out an authentic reaction. However, her response remained steadfast, delivered with her flawlessly curved lips, "*I'm sorry, I just don't seem to feel anything*," she uttered, her radiant smile unyielding.

Dealing with divas was a task in itself: consider the case of a fiery redhead with lavender eyes, notorious for her quick temper. The latest trigger was a delayed check from an advertising agency. Her explosive outburst included stomping, screaming, and causing a scene in the office. Walter, well-prepared for her tantrum, put on his own dramatic display: yelling, clearing his desk with a dramatic sweep of his hand and invoking the universe's fury against advertising agencies. He stormed out, leaving the shocked woman to retreat.

As anticipated, her check arrived that night. Walter brought her back to the office and, along with the check, gave her a stern talking-to. He emphasized her exceptional beauty but warned that her unchecked anger would tarnish her looks over time, leading to a hardened appearance that makeup couldn't conceal. She tearfully acknowledged the truth, pleading for a chance to change. Walter granted her that chance, setting her on a path of transformation. She was assigned rigorous exercises, including practicing various smiles in front of a mirror. Through dedication, Lola Martin, once a tempestuous diva, evolved into one of the industry's most sought-after cover girls.

Then there was the case of Lynn March. Despite her stunning looks, a past love affair had shattered her self-confidence, leaving her timid and nervous. Walter, recognizing her potential, invited her to a party where she observed the natural charm of successful individuals. Following his advice, Lynn transformed from a nervous wreck to a confident, engaging beauty. Attending subsequent gatherings, she blossomed into the dazzling model which led her to nonstop success.

In addition, there existed demands for models with very specific character traits that proved challenging to fulfill. A prime example was the client seeking a bearded male model to feature in their upcoming product advertisement. Exhaustively scouring his numerous catalogs and engaging in a series of phone calls, Walter eventually stumbled upon the ideal candidate—a bearded man stationed at a street corner, begging. Walter extended an offer of ten dollars for the assignment and an opportunity of becoming a model (a sum equivalent to over $200 by today's standards). However, the man politely declined, asserting that his earnings from begging surpassed the offer on the table.

So, yes, Dad had his hands full in those glamorous surroundings. Managing hundreds of beautiful girls. Developing and maintaining relationships with powerful clients. Establishing his agency as the first choice for those clients instead of his competitors. Keeping his agency and his girls in the press. He was under constant pressure to find, train, and transform more models and to make them successful to replace the ones who were leaving the modeling life. Heck, just dealing with the personalities and competitiveness of so many beautiful women could be a delicate balancing act by itself! It seems to me that Dad may very well have had the world's toughest job. Glamorous, yes, but tough!

Chapter 12

The Solo Shot Photo

Adriana

N ancy texted me at work early one morning, not long after we'd really started trying to figure out the "bankrupt investor" image. Her text just said, "CALL ME". I did right away.

"You're not going to believe this," she said, *"but there are <u>two</u> car photos. I think I'm so used to seeing that image in sort of icon-sized versions, I've never realized that there are actually two different poses of the photo. I just zoomed in on this second pose. Dad is the only guy in this one. It looks like he's talking on a cellphone, which we know was not possible in 1929,"* she said. *"I'm sending it to you right now."*

Above: Officially captioned "Man Selling Roadster After Stock Market Crash—Bankrupt investor Walter Thornton tries to sell his luxury roadster for $100 cash on the streets of New York City following the 1929 stock market crash"

"*Just got it,*" I said. "*I can't believe we never noticed. What is he doing in that photo? Scratching his head?*" "*This one shows more of the background buildings,*" Nancy said. "*Maybe we can use those to pinpoint the location where these pictures were taken. You can even see the license plate in this second image. Maybe we can find an address on one of the buildings.*"

In the solo image he has sort of a blank, unfocused expression which we took to be the sense of embarrassment he must have felt, to be faced with such a public calamity. He seems to have lost some of the stoic bravado he showed in the group shot. Recalling what a "car guy" our dad had been, constantly tooling with and babying his beloved, powder-blue, 1956 Cadillac in Ajijic, having to basically give away the grand motorcar in the images would have been devastating for him. Maybe the shock had set in by this point. His facial expression is hard to interpret. Sad? Confused? Resigned? Lost?

One of the first things we felt was important for us to do was to establish the location where the car photos had been taken, which was made possible with this newly realized solo image. Judging by the online suppositions of internet sleuths, the photos were taken...*where?* Does anybody really know? On Wall Street? Somewhere in New York City? As far as we could tell, no one had ever conclusively determined exactly where or when the two photos had been taken—or by whom. Or why. There is no credited photographer, source, *confirmed* date—or set of extant negatives. The only given provenance as to the two images is that they had been part of the photo collection of the Bettmann Archive, which then changed hands several times, before ultimately being subsumed by Getty Images.

Around 2010, after we'd been compelled to set aside our research into our father's past (more on that later), we slowly edged back into our project by regularly Googling Walter Thornton. In the intervening years since we'd abandoned our research mission, there was now much more information online related to Walter Thornton. Especially his famous car photos. When Google began offering Reverse Image Search in 2011, I typed "stock market crash 1929" and clicked "image search" and actually gasped aloud. The search results brought up a ton of online usages of the photos, from around the world. In only five years' time since we first spotted the photo in *Seabiscuit*, the two photos had evidently become American history icons. And we're not talking about long-defunct Myspace chat rooms, either. We're talking about the *New York Times*, the *Wall Street Journal*, PBS and History.com.

Pinpointing the exact location of the car photographs proved to be much easier than we expected (for a change). It was as plain as if it were displayed for us in a storefront window—which, in fact, it was. I zoomed in on the shop window directly behind and to the right in the solo image. I clearly made out the name "John G. Kelly." Cross-referencing a digitized copy of a Manhattan telephone directory from 1929, John G. Kelly was a plumber/electrician whose business was located at 210 East 45th Street in Midtown Manhattan, near the southeast corner at Third Avenue.

We further confirmed the location by visiting the site in-person, in 2022. In the solo image, of all the buildings shown in the background, only one of them remains standing. Fortunately, that building had a distinctive architectural feature: the lintels surrounding its windows. The 1929 photos perfectly match the still-extant windows. This final building seems to be in peril of demolition, too, so we were relieved to have seen this last-standing proof of 'bankrupt investor's" shooting location. (A researcher at the Library of Congress Prints & Photographs Division later reached the same conclusion, definitively confirming our research results.)

The car does bear a 1929 New York license plate, which places the photo in (or after) 1929. As the car is parked across the street from John Kelly plumbing and electric which means the car, the photographer and subjects would have been situated in front of 213 East 45th Street—an address we later learned came prominently into play in our father's life. And it had nothing to do with him publicly hawking his car on the street there, bemoaning his spendthrift failure on Wall Street. That was directly in front of Walter Thornton & Co., also known as the Walter Thornton head factory, which continued churning out perfect plaster copies of our father's much-exalted head until at least 1931. They were sold for six dollars apiece, C.O.D. ($100 according to the 2023 CPI).

We then confirmed that the very high-end car in the photo was a 1929 Chrysler Imperial 75 Roadster. It was one of Chrysler's top-of-the-line, luxury models that year. A wild coincidence, considering that our father was one of the first tenants in the Chrysler Building, that our father later became forever paired in the public consciousness with that splendid Chrysler motorcar. The detailing of the 1929 Chrysler Imperial 75 Roadster was unique to that year and model. Most notable was the double-winged radiator cap (hood ornament). It's gone down in history, actually. That design was replicated in stainless steel, by the Chrysler Building's architect, William van Alen, used as the prominent thirty-first-floor parapet adornments. Elements of that model's hubcaps and bumpers are also reimagined on the Chrysler Building's thirty-first floor edifice. What's more, the '29 Imperial 75 Roadster was a special beast in that Chrysler only manufactured 6,414 of that model that year.

It has become something of a New York urban myth that the Chrysler Building and the Empire State Building sat empty for years after they opened at the dawn of the Great Depression. While the Empire State Building (known in the early 1930s as the "Empty State Building") did have a low occupancy rate in its early years of operation, the Chrysler Building was not, in fact, under-populated. A large percentage of its offices were filled by the Texaco Corporation. Chrysler, itself, occupied the second largest bloc of tenancy. The building's respectable occupancy rate might also have been due to the building's generous incentives to new tenants willing to commit to longer-term leases.

We've found evidence, in the newspaper, that our dad signed a two-year lease, with rent "deferred" for his first five months of tenancy and later renewed it twice, which leads us to believe our dad got into the Chrysler Building at exactly the right moment in time—no money up front, rent-free until March 1931—in what was then the tallest building in the world. And, though raised in Mexico, even *we* knew what the Chrysler Building was when we were kids. Our dad kept a small, framed photo of it in his office. I once asked him, "*Papi, what is that building?*"

It seemed to glow like some mystical spire. *"It's a special building in New York. It was once the tallest building in the world, but only for a year...until the Empire State Building opened in 1931. I worked there once, the year that it was the world's tallest,"* he said, with his usual oversized dose of understatement.

Our main confusion surrounded the utter dichotomy between "bankrupt investor" and how all the newspaper articles we were finding about him painted him as a brilliant success story. He was one of John Robert Powers' most popular male models in 1929. Within months of Black Tuesday, Walter Thornton branched out and quickly became Powers' key competitor. Where did he find the time to go bankrupt?

"What if we could trace the license plate and prove the car didn't belong to him?" Nancy texted me in 2020.

"Let me work on that," I texted back. I'd wondered about that myself.

If we could prove the car did not belong to our father and was, in fact, owned by someone else, the presumed legitimacy of the photos would be an open and shut case: This tableau is not to be taken literally, since one cannot sell what one does not own. That was what we thought: Solve that riddle and you'll have your solid, indisputable proof that these images were not a biographical depiction of our dad.

I phoned the New York State Department of Motor Vehicles and actually reached a live person who informed me that the New York DMV did not keep accurate data records on license plates and their owners, pre-1930. In order to trace New York State licensing records going back as far as 1929, one needs the Vehicle Identification Number (VIN), which is usually located in a given car's interior. Well, the resolution of the image wasn't *that* good. So, that potential lead turned into yet another dead end.

We joined various websites and social media groups, related to antique automobiles, antique license plates, Chrysler collectors, Chrysler Imperial collectors. There's even a group that's specifically all about 1929 Chrysler Imperial 75 Roadsters. Our hopes were high that we might even be able to track down the very car in the images, if it still exists. More dead ends. We're still hoping, in fact, to learn of some secret channel into tracing 1929 New York license plates. The plate on the Chrysler reads "R3 7244 NY 29." One license plate collector we met online told us (unconfirmed) that the "R3" would signify the car was registered in Nassau County (Long Island, NY). There is no record of Walter Thornton ever living or working on Long Island for any period in his life. In 1929, he lived in the flat on MacDougal Street in Greenwich Village, Manhattan, which is in New York County. No census records tied him to being a resident of Nassau County, ever.

One thing we definitely had on our side in this particular quest was the enormous volume of existing information related to our father and his early career, verifying where he was and what he was doing in the years surrounding the stock market crash of 1929. He was acknowledged in his day as something of a master showman and promoter. Hence, he was widely written about in the press from the 1930s to the 1950s. "Beauty Impresario Walter Thornton," one tabloid columnist called him, as early as 1931.

Chapter 13

The Fairest in the Land

Nancy

So rapid was Walter's rise to being the National Beauty Expert, that he was chosen to be a judge in two consecutive Miss America contests in Atlantic City during 1933 and 1935, and later, a third one in 1947. (There was no pageant in 1934, for reasons which will be explained.) When Dad wasn't judging Miss America, he was constantly judging other pageants. Prior to 1933, there hadn't been a Miss America contest for a few years.

The pageant had been shuttered since 1928, largely owing to the stock market crash of 1929 and the resultant Great Depression. The 1933 pageant was looked upon as a "revival" of the contest—and it did not go well at all. It was, in fact, one of the most infamous show-business fiascos of the early twentieth century. It came close to being the last Miss America Pageant, had it not been for the judges (including Walter Thornton) uniting and collectively "going rogue" against mob racketeers.

Above: The panel of seven judges for Miss America, 1933 (and others) Standing, L to R Artist Peter Arno, Miss America producer Armand T. Nichols, illustrator Russell Patterson, Model King Walter Thornton, artist George Bucher, Drs. Edward Coward and David Allman Seated, L to R Beauty impresario George White (George White's Scandals), Ziegfeld beauty Gladys Glad, artist Hugh Walter (Photo: New York Daily Mirror)

The former Ziegfeld star showgirl, Gladys Glad (Our dad's beauty advise was often featured in her newspaper column), was the sole female judge of that year's pageant. Emerging from her limousine and floating through the lobby of Atlantic City's luxurious Ritz-Carlton, Miss Glad was surrounded by assistants, who were tasked with assignments such as caring for her multiple Pekingese...whenever cameras weren't around, that is.

She was accompanied by her husband, Mark Hellinger, the noted Broadway columnist, though few people seem to have taken notice of him. The other six judges were housed in the similarly plush, if less-exclusive boardwalk hotel, The Ambassador, in order to keep them separate from the contestants. Befitting her station as "America's Most

Beautiful Woman", Gladys was a total diva, played by her own rules, and had little interest in trivialities like schedules and punctuality.

Proof of this can be found in a local article at the time titled "Judges Are Late". And it foretold the many messy things to come:

"More than an hour late in starting because Gladys Glad, one of the judges, is not much of an early riser, the judging got off to a bad start when 'Miss New York State,' who is otherwise Miss Florence Meyers, collapsed after passing through the line of judges and spectators yesterday morning."

It happened in a preliminary round of the competition with the judges seated on the stage, their backs to the audience, that Miss New York State, the "19-year-old brunette of East Rockaway, Queens" fell to the floor of the stage in a dead faint, quite literally at the feet of our father and the other six judges. Some of the startled judges reportedly leapt from their seats to the aid of Miss Meyers. A well-rested Gladys Glad screamed, dramatically.

Pageant staff had Miss New York quickly and gently removed from the stage and into a waiting ambulance. It was hardly a secret that Miss Meyers was the favorite to win, so she was handled with care. Because if Nucky Johnson had his say in the matter—and he usually did—she was "it" that year.

Mob boss Enoch "Nucky" Johnson and his gang had maintained a stranglehold on the Miss America contest for years. Nucky saw to it that Miss New York State recovered quickly enough to return for the next day of competition. It was announced that her fainting was related to a recent emergency tooth removal. Another judge, noted illustrator and designer, Russell Patterson, waited twenty years before he felt safe enough to talk about the aura of coercion that had permeated the week-long event. He recalled the judges reeling from a series of misfires and bizarre happenstances that continued to unfold daily.

To begin with, Miss Oklahoma was forced to withdraw from the contest, due to an attack of appendicitis. Soon after, three other contestants (Misses Idaho, Iowa and Illinois) were sent packing when it was discovered that they did not, in fact, live in the states they were representing. The *Philadelphia Inquirer* would refer to the three banished, non-resident contestants as "The Three 'I' League."

The actual number of contestants dwindled by one more, when 'Miss' Arkansas was discovered to be a 'Missus.' Even crazier, the disqualified contestants were still allowed—and some of them quite willing—to participate in the pageant, in spite of understanding that they could not be advanced to the title of "Miss America." The pageant brass likely wanted to keep them around since, in the end, there were only thirty eligible contestants left in the running.

It's pretty telling, and pretty fishy, that these young contestants were being housed at the Ritz-Carlton—the very place to which one of the most notorious gangsters in America had a virtual master key. Nucky Johnson's suite occupied nearly an entire upper floor of that hotel. It had been an unspoken understanding throughout the 1920s that Johnson had a habit of trying to "convince" the judges as to who should receive the crown. And if his name rings a bell to you, it's because you probably watched the fictionalized version of the life of Nucky Johnson in the HBO series, *Boardwalk Empire.*

Russell Patterson recalled, in 1955:

"I was in the lobby of the Ambassador Hotel with another first-time judge, artist Peter Arno, when we were buttonholed by two rough-looking agents from Johnson's office. 'This is the name of the winner Johnson wants you to pick,' they said, flaunting a piece of paper at us. 'If you know what's good for you, you'll vote for this girl.' When Arno and I became indignant, they said, 'Look, that's the way we run the contest down here.'"

The behind-the-scenes arm-twisting by Johnson's thugs became so blatant, according to Patterson, that just two days before the official crowning ceremony, the seven judges had formulated a plan to resign *en masse.* They released the following statement, "We, as a panel, deem none of the contestants in this contest worthy to wear the crown of Miss America." The judges were somehow convinced by Pageant Director Armand T. Nichols to see the contest through to completion. At that point in the competition, the judges actually began to fear for their own safety—just as Nucky's "lobbyists" intended.

Saturday night, September 9, 1933, was the main event: the crowning of Miss America. The gigantic Atlantic City Convention Hall filled with the sounds of the world-famous "Million-Dollar Pipe Organ". The audience was asked to rise for the playing of the national anthem. The enormous musical instrument swept into a pull-out-all-the-stops arrangement of "The Star-Spangled Banner" before completely breaking down just ten bars into it ("Whose broad stripes and bright...."—*groaning halt*). The audience didn't know quite what to do as the hall fell silent and attendees awkwardly sat back down. Things only went downhill from there.

Russell Patterson also admitted that four of the judges had made a secret pact to select a neutral contestant, thus shutting out "Nucky's girl."

And the winner is... At the end of the ponderously long ceremony, when emcee Norman Brokenshire revealed that the winner that year would be Miss Connecticut, Marian Bergeron (the judges' "neutral" choice), the partisan audience exploded into a chorus of boos, whistles, catcalls and hissing, mostly from the front section of the crowd, which was heavily papered with Nucky Johnson's people. Judge George White had cast his final vote and made tracks, departing before the votes had even been tabulated. He'd done his job and had no desire to run into Nucky Johnson in a dark, Atlantic City alley.

There was a somewhat hastily assembled crowning of the new Miss America, upon which Norman Brokenshire drew the event to a speedy, awkward conclusion. By the end of the evening, they'd fixed the "Million-Dollar Organ" in order to provide a peppy exit medley of songs from the recent film hit *42nd Street.*

Above: Bottom center Quickly crowned Marian Bergeron, Miss Connecticut; to her left, first runner-up, Miss New York State; Top left Russell Patterson; Bottom left Judge Gladys Glad; Top right Walter Thornton; Bottom right A highly nervous Armand T. Nichols, perhaps waiting for Nucky

As a couldn't-be-more-appropriate ending to the chaotic pageant, it was discovered the following day that the freshly crowned winner of the title of Miss America 1933, Marian Bergeron, had falsified her age as sixteen. In fact, she was only fifteen-and-one-half-years old upon her coronation, rendering her too young to eligibly wear the crown of Miss America. Even so, Director Nichols ruled, without explanation, the judges' choice would prevail. It seems likely that Nichols just wanted this nightmare to end, and didn't have it in him to hold the contest all over again.

And since Nucky's choice, Miss New York State, had ended up as first runner-up, nullifying the judges' first choice would have essentially handed victory to Nucky Johnson. Their decision was final: Marian Bergeron would keep her crown. It's absolutely fitting with the shenanigans of the rest of the week that her bejeweled crown was stolen from her Ritz-Carlton hotel suite the same night she won it, never to be seen again.

The final vote count, by the way, was Miss Connecticut, four votes, Miss New York, two votes, and Miss California, one vote. We don't have conclusive proof of which contestant our father voted for, though all signs point to him voting with the Miss Connecticut bloc. After all, a month later our father and Russell Patterson worked together to fight for better wages for photographic models.

Interestingly, Walter Thornton was the *only* one of the 1933 judges who was asked to return to the following contest, which was held in September of 1935. There was no Miss America 1934. The organizers of the pageant had taken a year's hiatus to completely re-work the contest, from top to bottom—free from the constraints of Nucky Johnson and his gang. The 1935 contest rules and eligibility requirements were drastically improved.

They even added the "Talent Competition" to the Miss America contest that year (unleashing years and years of unfortunate operatic sopranos, tap-dancers and baton-twirlers upon the American public). Our dad is seen in frequent tabloid coverage of the event that year, looking glowingly handsome in his white linen summer suit, sporting a deep, Bermuda tan. By the early 1940s, he had judged more than two hundred pageants and contests.

Chapter 14

A Friend of Mine with a Knack for Nicknames

Adriana

Another question we had was how did Dad not only keep afloat, but achieve such success during the Great Depression years? One of the most helpful websites to us in our research has been Newspapers.com. As it continues to add more and more individual newspapers to its searchable archives, we've been able to assemble hundreds—perhaps thousands—of articles that either mention, or were written about, and by, Walter Thornton. Going through the newspapers from that era, we got quite an education of what was happening in America at the time. The differences were startling: images of destitute people lining up outside soup kitchens and articles advising ways to stretch a dollar would be on the same page next to illustrated ads showing beautiful women with copy urging the reader to buy the dress, own the lipstick, get the latest hat before it's gone. But, with the context that history gives, perhaps that contrast is not so surprising.

In a depressed economy where lavish excess was no longer possible, beauty was even more important to strive for than ever. The beauty industry had really taken off throughout the 1920s, and surprisingly, it grew by leaps and bounds in the 30s, almost in defiance of the Great Depression. In economic circles it's actually known as "the lipstick effect". It was the same with movie theaters. In 1931 the average ticket at the local movie house was twenty-five cents and lipstick from a value-line company would run you about thirty-nine cents. So, for well under a dollar, you could escape the desperate reality of the streets and walk into a glamorous film world. And look prettier while doing it.

Beauty sold, hence Walter's models had work. In fact, his agency employed dozens of young women who had lost their jobs after the stock market crash. Modeling for product advertisements actually provided a very comfortable living for all the different "types" that Walter represented. Even kids. During our research we met Tracie Townsend who is the daughter of a former child model. Her mother worked as a kid model in 1933 and continued into her teenage years. She looked a bit like Shirley Temple and was the primary source of income that supported her family during this time. And through our journey of research we have found numerous descendants of other child models who worked with Dad's agency.

As part of President Roosevelt's New Deal to restart the Depression economy, the National Recovery Administration (NRA) agency worked with leaders in different industries, establishing codes to keep competition fair and protect workers by regulating minimum wages and maximum working hours. Modeling, though, didn't fall neatly within the NRA's covered categories. So Walter, together with illustrator Russell Patterson and other artists and models, lobbied the NRA to recognize modeling's status as a career field and pushed for an agreement to set standards for fairer compensation.

At the time, commercial models were paid directly by ad agencies, often without reference to the value of the artwork or the ad campaign itself. Walter argued that a high-visibility campaign with a wide reach should be compensated at a higher rate than a photo shoot with a local or limited reach, especially since higher exposure often shortened a model's career by making her face too common and, thus, overexposed to readers.

Though the advocacy was unsuccessful (and the NRA declared unconstitutional within a few years), Walter had exposed a flaw in the modeling world: in many cases, modeling was by nature not a long-term career, particularly for women. A female model could do well if she stuck it out for as long as five years, though she and her agent would have to carefully choose her jobs so as not to overexpose her. Ironically, the more popular the model, the more quickly she hastened the end of her posing. Once her features became too recognizable, or she became popularly associated with a brand or a magazine, then advertisers, ever on the lookout for novelty, might seek talent elsewhere.

We repeatedly came across the term "The Merchant of Venus," which was often grafted onto our dad's name starting in the early 1930s. We were aware by this point in our research that "The Merchant of Venus' was a play on words, based upon the title of the Shakespearean play, *The Merchant of Venice*, but we were still puzzled by exactly how the "Merchant of Venus" moniker came to be and where it came from. It turns out he'd been granted the flattering, publicity-ready nickname by no less than famed gossip columnist Walter Winchell.

With a syndicated readership somewhere in the tens of millions, you couldn't hope for anything better to promote your business in the 1930s than to land a mention in Winchell's column. Those lucky enough to have their name and image printed in a Winchell column could leverage the exposure into career-making good fortune. The other side of that coin, though, were the people who fell into Winchell's disfavor and suffered his wrath in the column. Those poor schmucks could very likely kiss their careers goodbye. Winchell was one of Walter Thornton's earliest, most vocal supporters. He first mentioned Walter Thornton in his *New York Daily Mirror* column in 1931.

Winchell, it seems, had previously used the Merchant of Venus term as early as 1929 to describe another beauty impresario of the 1920s and 30s, Earl Carroll, who, among other things, was a theatrical producer and worked with beautiful girls. For whatever reason, it didn't seem to "stick" with Earl Carroll (or, perhaps, Carroll somehow fell from favor, which was always a possibility with Winchell). So, clearly proud of the clever Shakespeare-influenced turn of phrase, Winchell decided to revive the name and gave it to the up-and-coming new kid in town, Walter "The Merchant of Venus" Thornton.

In a 1936 interview distributed by King Features Syndicate, titled, 'The Trials of a Merchant of Venus,' our father was asked directly, "*Where did you get the name 'Merchant of Venus'?*" Walter replied, "*Oh, a friend of mine with a knack for nicknames.*"

As we said earlier, any press is good press and while I'm certain that our dad appreciated the many mentions in Winchell's column, some of the "quotes" Winchell attributed to our dad through the years seem a little far-fetched, like this one from Winchell's October 25, 1932 column, "On Broadway," in the *New York Daily Mirror:*

"Walter Thornton tells it on Will Grefé, the famous artist, who is absent-minded when he paints. A model was posing in the lewd, the windows were wide open, there was no steam heat, and the day was icy. The shivering model could stand the cold blasts no longer and hinted: 'Don't you find it chilly in here?'

'Chilly?' said Grefé, coming out of his trance, 'Why, so it is. 'Scuse me a moment.' And so saying, he left the studio, came back attired in his overcoat and resumed."

That doesn't remotely sound like something our dad would have said but go ahead.

As Winchell was never a big one on fact-checking, there were often mistakes in his column. One hit close to home when our enigmatically named half-sister, Daryl, was born in 1935 and Winchell announced, "*It's a lad* in the Walter & Judy Thornton household". (Winchell corrected the error in his column the following day.) It would probably be stretching the truth to refer to the two Walters as "friends". From all we've gathered, it seems they were more like *frenemies.* A suitable word choice since the term "frenemy" has become perhaps the most enduring of all Winchellisms. Walter Winchell first coined it in 1952—in relation to the United States and the Soviet Union's tenuous relationship.

The more we learned about the mercurial Walter Winchell, the more amazed we were to learn that our father seemed to have somehow stayed in Winchell's good graces for nearly thirty years.

In addition to "The Merchant of Venus", other descriptive titles Winchell and the other columnists applied to Walter Thornton were "Model Man, Walter Thornton," "Model Maestro," "The Model King," "Pin-Up King Walter Thornton" and "Beauty Expert Walter Thornton."

I n the latter 1930s, our father had his own beauty advice column that was widely distributed by King Features Syndicate. We found a few editions in the boxes. It was called "At the Court of the Merchant of Venus." The columns were written by Walter "The Merchant of Venus" Thornton, with each one focused on different beauty-centric topics. We also found an earlier column written by him in the mid-1930s, also distributed by King Features, titled 'The Trials of a Merchant of Venus,' where he talks about his job managing the world's most beautiful girls.

Not content with just printed media, Walter Thornton had a radio program called—of course—*The Merchant of Venus*, from 1937 to 1940 (there are no known surviving scripts or aircheck recordings). The fifteen-minute radio programs were hosted by Walter and his first wife Judy, who was always referred to, in the style of the day, as Mrs. Walter Thornton.

The shows were live broadcasts from their deluxe penthouse suite at the Mayflower Hotel, which stood near the southwestern corner of Central Park West at Central Park South. Other beauty experts appeared on the weekly panel, to quiz the Walter Thornton beauties on beauty-related topics; also offering common-sense advice on cosmetics, style, fashion and demeanor. The popularity of his radio show led to the CBS network offering him the opportunity to headline one of the earliest, self-named, celebrity television shows, in 1946, The *Thornton Show*. Hosted by Mrs. Walter Thornton, the show went beyond just talking about beauty applications. With the benefit of TV, it conducted the first "how-to" demonstrations on makeup applications for a television viewing audience. The Walter Thornton pinups were regularly featured.

The Thornton Show 1940

For years, in the late 1930s through the mid-1940s, the list of "Best-Dressed Businesswomen in America", given by The Fashion Academy, always included the name Mrs. Walter Thornton. Societal regulations of the day were so rigid that it took us a long time to finally learn her first name: Judith "Judy" Dolan, née Dolinsky. They met because she was a Walter Thornton model. They were married for nearly twenty years. We knew that the woman we were once introduced to as our sister, Daryl, really was our half-sister but in our minds, she was relegated to the "do not even try to process" file. I mean, how could this much-older American woman be our *sister?* When we eventually did our math we found that Daryl Virginia Thornton was actually born *two years before our mother was.*

She was a bit of a shadowy figure during our childhood years, but in a benevolent way. I always thought she was so pretty. She traveled to Ajijic periodically during our childhood and we were aware our father had visited her in the States on occasion. She was kind and radiated warmth toward all her half-siblings. The final time we ever saw her was briefly at our father's funeral in 1990. She was seated across the church with her daughter, Lucienne, our half-niece, whom we'd never met (but with whom we are now close). We didn't see Daryl after that. We found out, years after the fact, that she had been killed in a 1996, single-car accident, on a deserted highway outside of Santa Fe, New Mexico. The coroner later ruled it to have been caused by some sort of medical event while driving, likely cardiac arrest.

Above: (L) Walter and first wife Judy (R) Daryl Virginia Thornton and her daughter Lucienne Lightfoot.

Chapter 15

The Brooklyn Bombshell, the Fallen Starr and other Discoveries

Nancy

"There is no formula for making discoveries. Finds come in the most curious disguises."–Walter Thornton

Those born in the United States have a much firmer grasp on American popular culture than we Thornton children had, growing up in Ajijic. All we knew about U.S. culture came to us as filtered through our father's tutelage and a little TV. One name that definitely rang a bell for us, and just about everyone else, was Flash Gordon. The character of Flash initially started from the sketchpad of comic strip artist Alex Raymond. Raymond was an on-staff artist at King Features Syndicate. In late 1933 his bosses tasked him to come up with a Sunday feature comic strip to compete against the National Newspaper Syndicate's "Buck Rogers" strip. On January 7, 1934, "Flash Gordon' debuted.

The story setup went something like this: Earth is on a collision course with planet Mongo. So Dr. Zarkov plans to take his rocket ship to the planet and find a way to divert it from crashing into Earth. Half-crazed with the responsibility of his mission, and perhaps a little lonely, he kidnaps Yale graduate and polo player, Flash Gordon, as well as pretty Dale Arden. Once landed on Mongo, our three heroes engage in unending battles with Mongo's ruler, Ming the Merciless.

It was the Walter Thornton Agency that supplied model Patricia Quinn to Alex Raymond for the drawing and development of Flash's one true love, Dale Arden. And evidently, she wasn't the only model from Dad's agency to work with Raymond on characters for the comic strip. It would be amazing if we were ever to find out that our dad supplied a male model to create Flash, himself! In any case, Flash Gordon would far surpass Buck Rogers. In addition to the three different film serials, radio and TV versions, that original Sunday strip, which began in 1934, continued uninterrupted until 2003.

Above: Alex Raymond sketches Thornton model, Patricia Quinn, for the character of Dale Arden in the Flash Gordon comic strip, 1933.

Dad has been associated with many later-famous names but perhaps the earliest model he represented that would gain notoriety was more infamous than famous, and it's the saddest story we know.

Other than Walter himself, Starr Faithfull became the first head-line-making model in the early 1930s. She was born Marian Starr Wyman, adopting her middle name and the last name of her stepfather, Stanley Faithfull, in 1925. The Thornton Agency represented her and her sister Tucker in the first year it was open for business. Starr possessed a remarkable beauty. She was described in a June 12th 1931 article from the New York *Daily News* as having brown, wavy hair, brown eyes, and exquisitely crafted features.

Although we encountered difficulty in locating photographs of her within our father's archives, her captivating beauty is vividly evident in the pictures that appeared in the newspapers of that era. But not long into her association with the agency, she had perfected her growing reputation as a "party girl" and that was the last thing that was tolerated at the Walter Thornton Agency. Walter noted that her career as a model had largely come and gone; her face (and tabloid reputation) was overly exposed, and artists and photographers were just no longer booking her.

Then, on June 8, 1931, the battered corpse of a beautiful, twenty-five-year-old washed ashore on a stretch of beach on Long Island. It was Starr. Her body was garbed in a silk printed summer dress, stockings and nothing else. It was presumed she had somehow drowned. An autopsy found she had recently ingested a large meal and a large amount of Veronal (a strong sedative available over the counter at that time).

The New York tabloid reporters sardonically chuckled that the autopsy results showed a zero percent blood alcohol content. Surely this was a first, they wrote, as her cocktail-fueled antics had become a mainstay in their publications. At first, it was presumed to be a suicide. Mental stability was not something Starr Faithfull was famous for. But was it suicide or murder?

As details of her life continued to pour out in the press, it was obvious to all why this poor young woman had lost her way. It was uncovered that, from the time she was eleven years old she had been sexually abused, on a continuing basis, by a middle-aged distant relative named Andrew Peters, during a period when he was the *Mayor of Boston*! Her parents somehow never caught on and continued letting their young daughter go on unchaperoned trips with His Honor, The Mayor.

For seven years. Rebelling from the emotional turmoil, Starr dropped out of high school and took to wearing boys' clothes to shroud her femininity. When, at age eighteen, she told her parents flat out what had been going on, they hired a lawyer who drafted an agreement for Peters to pay them $20,000 ($353,000 according to the 2023 CPI), supposedly for Starr's medical/psychiatric care, in exchange for their silence on the matter. But there were reports that just before her death, Starr's stepfather, Stanley Faithfull, had hit up Peters for another round of hush money.

Her death became—and remains—one of New York's most scandalizing unsolved deaths of the early twentieth century. Novelist John O'Hara later loosely based the character 'Gloria Wandrous' in his 1935 novel, *BUtterfield-8* on poor Starr. She was played by Elizabeth Taylor in the 1960 film version.

After her big sister's death, Tucker Faithfull continued to model under the Walter Thornton banner. With the settlement money having been spent in the intervening six years, the family was in financial straits and the income from her modeling helped support the family. Walter put a big effort into Tucker's promotion. The willowy doll-faced girl was transformed from a brunette to a blond and the agency took out full-page advertising in newspapers and magazines.

She was given a full page in the WTMA catalog. Unlike the other models though, Tucker's catalog page read "no underwear, corsets, etc.". To be successful, models needed to be able to pose for advertisements in all kinds of garments, including corsets, underwear and bathing suits. Her parents would not allow her to pose as such, given the circumstances of her sister's reputation and death.

For his part, Walter did all he could to change people's perceptions and get them to see her as a beautiful model and not merely the sister of a salacious headline. There were reports circulating in the columns that

Walter Thornton was dating Tucker. Was it true? It wouldn't surprise us. In 1931, our father was a famously handsome, twenty-eight-year-old bachelor. One of New York's most eligible suitors. They were both young, beautiful and single. Why not? Whether true or false, it would have been over by the first week of 1932, when he began dating his future wife, Judy Dolan.

Starr Faithfull's death remains officially unsolved.

S ince so many of the articles and photos we were uncovering mentioned other famous names that we didn't recognize, Adriana and I set out to give ourselves a crash course on the history of Hollywood and its movies, circa 1930-1955. When we scanned the early rosters of models under the Thornton banner, they were, for the most part, just names on a list. But as we started studying each of them, we learned that many of them went on to major careers as Hollywood stars, after getting their introductions to the world of glamour by the Walter Thornton Model Agency.

Some of his earliest stable of models-turned-Hollywood-actresses included:

Grace Bradley (co-star of Bing Crosby; she become Mrs. Hopalong Cassidy/William Boyd)

Boots Mallory (had an acting career; married James Cagney's brother, William, and retired)

Dorothy Dell (had a short acting career; killed when a drunken beau drove off a road in the Hollywood Hills in 1934)

Judith Allen (Paramount star; Cecil B. deMille gave her this name, without her knowledge)

Jean Muir (first performer to be blacklisted because of a mention in *Red Channels* in 1950)

Irene Ware (Princess Nadji in *Chandu The Magician* with Bela Lugosi and Edmund Lowe)

Adrienne Ames (1930s actress and wife of actor Bruce Cabot;1940s New York radio host)

Linda March (real-life sister of Adrienne Ames; killed in a car accident all too young in 1933)

Claudia Dell (can be seen in the film logo for Worldwide Pictures holding two globes, chest-high)

Charlotte Henry (known for notable films like the 1933 *Alice in Wonderland* with W.C. Fields, Cary Grant and Gary Cooper; selected from amongst 6,000 auditions)

Jean Muir modeled under her real name, Jean Fullarton, until 1933, when she signed a seven-year contract with Warner Brothers. Her career as a model was soon airbrushed from her resumé, establishing a pattern of things to come for Walter. Thornton had come to believe that "the model starlets of today will become the big stars of tomorrow... in modeling, stage, screen, radio and television." This idea went for kids as well. When Peggy Ann Garner was four years old, the Thornton Agency repped her as a child model in 1936 and 1937. She went on to enjoy teen and adult success in Hollywood: (*Jane Eyre* (1943), Academy Juvenile Award winner for *A Tree Grows in Brooklyn* (1945), *Teresa* (1951), *Black Widow* (1954), *The Cat* (1966), and *A Wedding* (1978).

Above: (L)The Thornton Agency's first major Hollywood crossover star, Jean Muir (1935) (R) Grace Kelly, early modeling photo (1954) (Wikipedia)

The former Thornton model who later attained the greatest international fame would have been Grace Kelly, when she became Princess Grace of Monaco in 1956. Studying images from her earliest days as an up-and-coming Broadway actress and Thornton model in the late 1940s, it is clear that she was loaded with "It" from the very start. She obviously wouldn't have needed much "remaking" at all. One of our dad's model scouts spotted her extraordinary potential in an off-Broadway play and brought her to Walter's attention.

He soon promoted her as one of his premier, most in-demand models. Grace was so popular as a model that she was chosen to be the cover model for top-selling *Redbook* magazine three times in less than one year. Kelly was one of Walter Thornton's final "major discoveries" as he began winding down his modeling agency in the late 1940s.

When Princess Grace was killed in a car wreck in 1982, it was a major story in every part of the world. Adriana and I recall watching Mexican news coverage of her state funeral from Monaco with our dad. He seemed uncharacteristically silent and sad as we watched her funeral cortege.

"I used to know her a long time ago. She was the real thing," he commented. We heard him use that term only sparingly. "The real thing." It was his highest compliment for someone he admired. *"You knew Princess Grace?"* I asked him. *"Well, I wouldn't say I 'knew' her, and it was long before she became a princess, but we worked together once,"* he replied. *"She was as beautiful inside as she was outside."*

In that same vein, another actress's death seemed to hit him particularly hard: the American actress Susan Hayward. The Oscar-winning star fought a very public battle with cancer, eventually succumbing to the disease in 1975. *"I worked with her once,"* he said. *"She was a good girl. Tougher than a cheap T-bone. She could—and would—chew you up and spit you right out...but I understood her. She had a hard life. I forgave her a long time ago."*

His recollections of Susan Hayward came rushing back to us when we finally opened that last box containing all our father's legal papers. We came upon a fairly weighty manila folder of items relating to "Edythe Marrenner" (the birth name of actress Susan Hayward). Magazine articles, newspaper articles, hand-written letters, signed contracts, many modeling photos, legal filings. He didn't just "work with her once" we soon learned: He actually discovered her. We can let our dad take over the narration of what happened next, as recounted by Walter Thornton in a 1940 article titled, "You, Too, Can Be Beautiful," from *New True Story* magazine:

"In some cases, it has been necessary to show girls in a way to overcome blemishes and handicaps. The story of Edith Marriner [One of several experimental spellings and variations on her name] is a case in point [...] Edith came to my office a few years ago without advance appointment [...] Gradually she told me her story. Her father was slowly dying from a defective heart. He was unable to work and had been out of a job for months. All his savings had been exhausted and he had only a few more weeks to live [...] It was a story of poverty and struggle.

"The only income of the family was the few dollars an older sister made working weekends in a millinery shop. The home conditions Edith revealed would have moved a heart of stone. She was on the verge of tears many times. There was pleading in her voice, pleading in her eyes. This girl was desperate for a job. Beneath her red, blotchy freckles I saw a clear ivory skin, and her red hair was the rarest asset of beauty in the world, for color photography was just coming into its own. Ignoring the freckles—just looking at the delicate contours of her sweet face beneath that mass of red gold that was her hair—she might have been a throwback to Venus.

"To put her mind at ease I said, "When do you want to start to work?" "Oh, Mr. Thornton," she said happily, "any time from now." "Then we'll start now," I told her. "We'll start with the make-up." My motion picture experience of years before had taught me many of the tricks of make-up. I obtained, and showed her how to use, a facial foundation. It was a heavy cream darker than her skin. It covered the freckles. We covered the foundation with powder."

He saw in this desperate young lady someone who just really needed a break. It seems obvious that young Edythe's ambition, in spite of the odds against her, was something that deeply touched our dad. In addition to her beauty, she had grit and nerve and, without a doubt, the fierce determination to succeed. Walter knew from the start that her natural red hair was her most-valued asset. He promptly sent her to the Thornton Agency's preferred hair stylist, a Mister Kent on East 56th Street.

Edythe's unprofessionally treated rusty red locks with the frizzy home permanent wave became a flaming mane of brilliant, Titian curls. The transformative effect was breathtaking. Walter was determined to find a better name for Miss Marrenner. She was Edith Marriner while under the aegis of the Thornton Agency. Six other separate variations were tried out when she decamped for Hollywood: Edythe Marriner, Edith Marriner, Susan Hayworth, Mary Hayward, Susan Heyward, then Susan Hayward—the name under which she became world-famous.

He fully believed (and said so in several interviews) he could make this young woman a star model. At just five foot three she'd certainly have been too short to be considered for fashion modeling. Live fashion shows would also have been out of the question, and not only because of her height. She had a discernible "wobble" in her walk from a childhood accident that stunted the growth of her right leg, making it nearly two inches shorter than the left one.

Dad stated in an article published in *True Story Magazine*, dated January 1940, "I taught Edith Marriner to walk gracefully, and here are the secrets of graceful walking: Balance, keeping along a straight line, swinging the arms from the shoulders, and placing the forward foot directly in front of the one behind it. The head should always be held erect."

What he didn't disclose is that it was his idea to get her fitted for a pair of orthopedic, height-correcting shoes. In her initial interview with Walter Thornton, she took out the crudely made, cardboard lift from her right shoe and tearfully demonstrated how impaired a gait she actually had. In most of his interviews about Susan Hayward, our father rather cagily discussed her "handicap", which was always implied to be her freckled face.

Their deal was inked on March 3, 1937. Edythe Marrenner (and her unpleasant stage mother, Ellen Marrenner) co-signed a three-year contract that also covered motion pictures, radio and stage in addition to modeling, with option to renew (we found the signed contract in our father's effects). He put her to work straightaway.

Above: A page from the Walter Thornton lookbook of 1937 featuring Edythe Marrenner (Susan Hayward)

In January of 1937, Walter was contacted by the *Saturday Evening Post*'s new editor, Wesley Winans Stout, about a proposed feature article on the life of the Merchant of Venus. What's more, they asked

Walter to write it himself. "The Merchant of Venus, by Walter Thornton," narrated in the first-person. During the first half of the twentieth century, the *Saturday Evening Post* was the most popular magazine in the world and the Halloween 1937 edition would be no less than the official anointing of Walter Thornton as *the* beauty powerhouse known as The Merchant of Venus.

During his career as a model, our father's face could frequently be found in images of *Saturday Evening Post* advertisements and fictional story illustrations. But now, as a featured *author* in the periodical, Walter Thornton joined a star-studded list of writers who had contributed stories to the magazine, including Mark Twain, F. Scott Fitzgerald, John Steinbeck, James Fenimore Cooper, Harriet Beecher Stowe, Washington Irving and Edgar Allan Poe. In short, a Who's Who of American writers of the nineteenth and twentieth centuries.

By 1937, advances in color photography paved the way for the future of print advertising. Because of this, redheads became all the rage in the late 1930s. And Walter's article would be the first in the magazine's history to feature accompanying color photographs. Through sheer fate, scrappy Edythe Marrenner's audition for the Walter Thornton Model Agency was a right-place, right-time event that resulted with her inclusion in the *Post*'s article. The article changed her life.

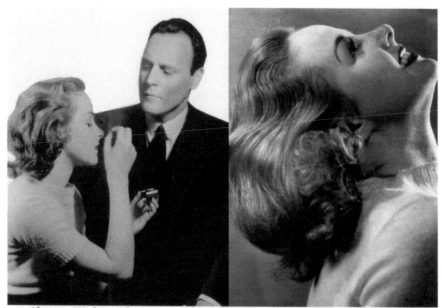

Above: Walter Thornton and Edith Marrenner (Susan Hayward)

In the immediate aftermath of the "Merchant of Venus" article in the *Saturday Evening Post*, the refreshingly beautiful and inexperienced model took the ball and ran down the field with it. She is named and quoted in the article. It was almost unheard of at that time for advertisement models to be identified at all. Suddenly Edythe's already-busy modeling calendar didn't show a single available minute. The article also generated a sizable show-business "buzz." Walter had chosen wisely. Unfortunately, however, his young protégé showed her hand by disappearing from the Walter Thornton Agency within weeks of the article's release. Contract or no contract. The twenty-year-old Edythe had been spotted in the *Saturday Evening Post* feature by the wife of an important Hollywood film producer.

But before she abandoned the agency, Walter secured a three-month contract for her and her sister Florence as "chaperone", to travel to Hollywood on a salary of $150 a week ($3140 according to the 2023 CPI), with an additional $100 for her sister and all expenses, so she could screen test for a role in an upcoming, much-anticipated feature film. According to some chroniclers of the film's history, she was actually an early, dark-horse favorite for the role, if only briefly. Walter Winchell even predicted she was an "odds-on favorite" to get the role. The director (before he was pushed out of the film) was George Cukor, and the producer was David O. Selznick. The role was Scarlett O'Hara, and the movie was *Gone with the Wind.* It was Selznick's wife, Irene Mayer Selznick, who'd seen the *Saturday Evening Post* article in the first place.

Edythe had gone from an unknown girl to one that everyone wanted. Walter said, in an interview for *Pic Magazine* on August 30, 1939, "*She had been turned down by every motion picture company in the East, Selznick included. When I asked them why they were so anxious to test a girl they had so definitely and coldly turned down just some months ago, they replied I had done something to the girl. She was suddenly beautiful.*" By the way, the scenario of being turned down by film studios before the "Walter Thornton Touch" made her suddenly desirable was not new. The very same thing had happened to Walter just five years earlier with the actress Judith Allen, who'd been 'given the go-by' from the movie companies until Walter's makeover made Cecil B. deMille take notice and star her in the 1933 hit, *This Day And Age.*

The "Search for Scarlett" campaign lasted for almost two years with nearly every actress under the age of forty being considered for the role. So they said. The endless publicity and anticipation lasted until January 13, 1939, when it was announced that British actress Vivien Leigh was the official choice to play the role. Walter later recounted the "tearful farewells from the train platform", as he and Judy saw Edythe off at Grand Central Station, heading to Hollywood. "In fact, that day was the only time I ever saw her express any emotion of any kind". Walter and Judy were happy that they had placed Edythe under option and hoped that she would get the role of Scarlett. "Did you know Winchell ran you in his column, as being the most likely prospect for the coveted role?" Walter wrote in a November 27, 1937 letter to her.

We also found several letters in the same folder as the "Merchant of Venus" *Post* article, between Walter and Edythe: hers chronicling how much she loved Hollywood; his always including encouraging words in his greetings. "*By the way, I still think Selznick is going to tap you to play Scarlett,*" he wrote in January 1938, along with subtle, friendly reminders that she was still his client. It was unbeknownst to Walter that she had been eliminated by then as a contender.

But since David O. Selznick had her under personal contract for a three-month period (on loan from the Thornton Agency), the studio made use of her and put her to work, reading with an endless stream of other potential performers, male and female, who were testing for various roles in the film—including the role of Scarlett. It's estimated that she appeared in over one hundred screen tests with other performers. Outtakes of some of her various screen tests have survived, and you can see that, whatever she was feeling, she was poised, focused and intense in her readings.

But on November 20, 1938, in one of his famous interdepartmental "Memos from D.O.S." Selznick officially vetoed her for any further consideration for the role, or anything else. Selznick wrote, "I think we can forget about Susan Hayward because we don't even need her any more as a stand-in for Scarlett, or to work with people we are testing for the other roles, what with others around." Ouch.

For their initial stay in town, Selznick had housed the Marrenner sisters in a suite at the Hollywood Roosevelt Hotel on Hollywood Boulevard. Edythe had excitedly written to the Thorntons that "you can even see the footprints at Grauman's Chinese Theater from my room!" [Fourteen years later, Hayward's own prints were added to Grauman's forecourt.] After being dropped by Selznick, the hotel was much too expensive for Edythe/Susan to foot the bill, so she and Florence took a place not far away in the Hollywood Dell section of town.

She stayed in touch with Walter at first, continuing to send breezy reports of her multiple screen tests and shopping at the Hollywood Farmers Market and picking oranges right off the trees. Meanwhile, and without the knowledge of Walter Thornton, she had signed with a Hollywood agent named Benny Medford for representation. Medford was able to wrangle her a six-month, one-hundred-dollar-a-week contract with Warner Brothers.

She somehow failed to mention that small fact in her cheery, but increasingly infrequent letters to Walter. Later, she would drop Medford like a hot rock when she was done with him, too. He was quoted in the newspapers saying: "This girl is smart, but cold as a polar bear's foot." Using today's jargon, you could say that Susan Hayward *ghosted* our dad. That's the best term I can think of to describe how she unceremoniously dumped Walter Thornton and his agency after he spent thousands of dollars to promote her, not to mention the time it took to transform her. And, perhaps saddest of all, the personal relationship and care that both Walter and Judy had lavished on her. They had really cared for that girl.

She simply "forgot" she had a signed contract with the Thornton Model Agency, which entitled the Thornton Agency to ten percent of any motion picture earnings until the end of that contract (which would have expired in 1940). Her blatant ignoring of numerous calls, letters and telegrams finally forced our father's hand. While briefly back in New York, Edythe/Susan paid an unannounced visit to the Walter Thornton Agency offices to say hello "to all my old pals," she later told the press. After having been completely incommunicado for almost a year, Walter was there to greet his former Venus with a "summons to appear".

He was suing her for $100,000 ($2.2 million according to the 2023 CPI) in lost potential income regarding her breach of contract. According to an article published in the *World Telegram*, October 24, 1939, an angry and defiant Hayward told a suite full of reporters, at New York's ritziest hotel, the Waldorf-Astoria: "$100,000 is a lot of money. I'm from Brooklyn, and he's not going to get one cent of it." Some weeks later, on Hayward's behalf in 1939, Paramount Studios settled an undisclosed amount with the Thornton Agency. It's a shame to think that the relationship was finished and settled so unpleasantly. It didn't have to end that way—though, perhaps, with Susan Hayward, it did.

Chapter 16

The Star Maker and his Femmes Fatales of Film Noir

Adriana

I n spite of the sour taste left by Susan Hayward's hasty departure (and subsequent legal actions), our father wasted no time dusting himself off and moving on. Ever since we started our dig into Hollywood history, I found myself especially drawn to film noir movies of the 1940s and 50s. Looking into our dad's "star discoveries," we viewed as many of their films as we could find and it dawned on us how many of our father's former models starred in classic Hollywood film noir movies.

The term "film noir" wasn't in common use back when these highly stylized melodramas were first being made (roughly early-1940s through mid-1950s). Though it was first coined in 1946 by the French film critic, Nino Frank, in a French publication, the term didn't become widely accepted by critics and film historians until the 1970s both in the U.S and Europe. In the twenty-first century, film noir has been elevated into a certified and distinct genre of its own: a very slick method of bare-bones storytelling—often on a shoestring budget.

Most typically, they were filmed in stark, shadowed black-and-white. They tended to feature variations of cynical detectives and the gorgeous temptresses that led them into some kind of ruin. A key feature is the *femme fatale*, which *Merriam-Webster* defines as "a seductive woman who lures men into dangerous or compromising situations: a woman who attracts men by an aura of charm and mystery."

Above: (L to R) Lauren Bacall, Hazel Brooks and Lizabeth Scott (Wikipedia)

Over a dozen former Thornton models appeared in films noir: Susan Hayward, Lauren Bacall, Lizabeth Scott, Hazel Brooks, Arlene Dahl, Celeste Holm, Dorothy McGuire, Dolores Donlon, Cathy Downs, Phyllis Brooks, Anita Colby, Suzy Parker, and Grace Kelly. Bacall and Scott were often mentioned together, comparatively, since they were the same angular, husky-voiced, "type." (You could really include Jean Muir on the list, too, since she made an early noir called *The Lone Wolf Meets a Lady* (1940). This would be a decade before her own noir-like takedown, when her name appeared in the McCarthy-era *Red Channels* blacklist publication in 1950).

Above: Undated, late-1940s advertisement brochure for the Thornton Agency, featuring Thornton's "all-stars" Clockwise from Top R: Lizabeth Scott; Walter Thornton with Cathy Downs; Dolores Donlon; Walter Thornton with Susan Hayward; Walter with five of his pinups, along with Bob Hutton, male model-turned WWII film star; Walter touches up the makeup of Lauren Bacall; Arlene Dahl in her "star-making" portrait; Dolores Donlon with Walter Thornton; popular film star Dorothy McGuire.

Our dad told a funny story in a fan magazine of how his seven-year-old daughter, Daryl, was actually the one who "discovered" Lizabeth Scott in 1942. Walter, Judy and Daryl Thornton were still living in the Mayflower Hotel penthouse on Central Park West. Lizabeth Scott (who was understudying Tallulah Bankhead on Broadway at the time) was living there as well. One evening, Daryl said to him, *"Daddy, I just found the perfect model for you, and she lives right here in the building."* Walter had just returned home after a long day and was harried and not in a good mood.

He replied, *"I've seen all the women in this building, and they all have bandy legs and buck teeth."*

"Not all of them, really," purred the husky voice of Lizabeth Scott, emerging from the shadowed seclusion of the Thornton's living room, where Daryl had hidden her.

He went on:

"I was horribly embarrassed. But she was so unruffled and good-humored, so completely charming that within five minutes, I felt I'd known her a lifetime. She had silky blonde hair, attractive dark eyes and an undisputed way with her. Probably you've heard of her. Her name? Lizabeth Scott."

The Walter Thornton Agency signed her to an exclusive modeling contract and she soon became a fixture in many of the high-fashion magazine ads and pictorials of the era. She was also billed as a "Walter Thornton Pin-Up" in several advertisements. Diana Vreeland, editor of *Harper's Bazaar* magazine, took special interest in the Thornton Agency's newest model—just as she had with Walter Thornton's previous star beauty, Lauren Bacall (and later, Arlene Dahl). And also like Lauren Bacall—and, for that matter, Susan Hayward—Lizabeth changed her name (dropping the "E" from Elizabeth), left modeling for good and made her way to Hollywood. Much the same way that Warner Bros. had nicknamed Bacall, The Look, Paramount bestowed on Scott the nickname, The Threat. And *the rest, as they say...*

Well into our research, we came across a 1942 photograph our father had saved in his files: It is a professionally posed shot of our dad, seated, observing a young woman named Betty Bacal, standing with, of all things, a book on her head:

Above: Walter Thornton's "It Girl" model of 1942-43, Betty Joan Perske/Betty Bacal/Lauren Bacall.

I'd been struck by one particularly cryptic comment he made in his later years that always stuck with me, something he once yelled at the TV in our family room in Ajijic. A movie came on, starring Humphrey Bogart and Lauren Bacall, the film, *To Have and Have Not* (1943). It was dubbed in Spanish, though you could still hear the English dialogue. When Bacall made her first appearance in the film, Dad laughingly snarled at the TV, in sort of a sing-song taunt that was certainly out of character for him, "*You're welcome, Betty Joan Perske!*" "*What do you mean, Papi? Who is Betty Joan Perske?*" I asked. "*Oh, nothing...just barking at the TV again,*" he said, never putting these vexing comments into context. And maybe it sounds odd but we never really pushed for answers or explanations; Papi was the boss. Turns out, our father had crowned her "Miss Greenwich Village" in 1942 and signed her to an exclusive contract with the Walter Thornton Model Agency directly following the pageant, the year before she exploded onto the Hollywood scene. Her success had been truly stratospheric. After she appeared on the cover of *Harper's Bazaar* in 1943, her modeling fee quintupled, overnight.

Hollywood director Howard Hawks and his wife, Slim Keith, spotted the striking Bacall magazine cover and swiftly whisked her to Hollywood, to screen test her opposite Humphrey Bogart for his upcoming film, *To Have and Have Not*. She was represented by the Thornton Agency for one year. Later, Bacall made half-hearted attempts at claiming that she was "never a model" early in her career. But in her autobiography, *By Myself,* she grudgingly gives Walter Thornton his due as her first—and only—modeling agent, as well as the man who crowned her "Miss Greenwich Village 1942". When Walter met her, she was going by the name of Betty Bacal—a shortened version of her grandmother's Roumanian maiden name, Weinstein-Bacal. She added the second "l" to her last name, because the other spelling was often mispronounced (rhymed with "jackal").

The label "model-denier" could not just be applied to Lauren Bacall and Susan Hayward. Nearly all of Walter's Hollywood star discoveries could be so branded. Thornton had complained about the "I was never a model!" trend as early as 1934, when he talked about "*the ingratitude of famous beauties who forgot their old maestro, once he started them to success,*" in a Hollywood fan magazine. There was a long-standing, and inaccurate, prejudice that all models are dim-witted and, thereby, only marginally talented, so the title of "former model" was one to be avoided by anyone seeking to build an acting career back in the day. One notable Thornton Agency discovery, the South African beauty Hazel Brooks, had a very brief, successful Hollywood career. Brooks was memorably cast as the beautiful, scene-stealing, second leading lady, opposite John Garfield, in *Body and Soul* (1947). Whenever she appeared onscreen, the film's actual leading lady, Lilli Palmer, seemed to fade into the background. Hazel Brooks had an aura that demanded the viewers' attention. Major "It". In a turnabout of the usual story, where Hollywood is quick to turn its back on its beauties, once done with them, Hazel Brooks was the one who turned *her* back on Hollywood for the role of Beverly Hills wife and society hostess.

One of Walter Thornton's most successful model-turned-Holly-wood-star moments happened in the waning days of WWII. She was a ravishing redhead who broke the mold of his prior model discoveries, in that she fully credited our father with her discovery. In several magazine interviews as early as 1950, Arlene Dahl gave our father credit for "putting me on the map." And we didn't just read about that. In 2019, we were able to get her mailing address through a mutual friend in New York City and contacted her, first via letter. We soon heard back from her very kindly assistant, Frankie Keane. It is not uncommon to find Arlene Dahl's name on lists of Hollywood's most beautiful actresses, ever. By the time we contacted her, she was happily married to her sixth and final husband, Marc Rosen. They shared a glamorous Fifth Avenue apartment overlooking Central Park at East 76th Street. Completing the circle, Arlene Dahl had posed for Georgia Warren early in her career, too (via the Thornton Agency).

"I've been lucky," she told *Modern Screen* magazine in a 1951 inter-view, "Lucky enough to be in the right place at the right time." She continued:

"I had to worry about finances only once—when 'Mr. Strauss Goes to Boston' folded." [That was Arlene Dahl's Broadway debut—which closed after just twelve performances in September of 1945.] "I was down to my last nickel when I appealed to Walter Thornton to help me get a job. I used to walk from 23rd Street to Central Park [...] and back again because I didn't have even bus fare. My shoes wore out, too. Plenty of matchbook covers have been scotch-taped into my inner soles."

Fast-forward seventy years. Upon finally making contact with Miss Dahl, we developed a tentative plan to fly to New York to interview her, in-person. Timing was not on our side, in that she received our letter just weeks before the COVID-19, pandemic-driven lockdown dashed our plans. After we didn't hear back from her for several months, we put together a Plan B. Considering Arlene Dahl was ninety-five years old when we first made contact, and knowing she was our father's very last living star model, there was an understandable urgency in our desire to interview her. Still though, we didn't want to be overly pushy or presumptuous. I suggested, "*Could we just submit a list of ten questions to you, by email?*" Ms. Dahl's assistant, Frankie, said that would be a perfect solution.

"*Walter Thornton! He got me my first modeling jobs in New York City. I haven't heard his name in many years. Whatever became of him?*" she asked in an email.

"*He closed his agency in the 1950s and moved to Mexico, where he raised six children, including myself,*" I replied by email. "*He left us in 1990.*"

"*Bless him. I remember Walter as a complete gentleman, and my first modeling agent. He got me a lot of jobs right away,*" she said. A striking, promotional shot of Arlene Dahl was released by the Thornton Agency the winter of 1945, just after WWII had drawn to a close. It made quite an impact and drew interest from Hollywood. We emailed her a copy of our father's own copy of the photo, which we found in one of his boxes in Ajijic. She seemed delighted to revisit this portrait that was crucial in getting her noticed by Hollywood. "*I don't even remember where we shot it. I haven't seen that one in ages!"* she wrote. *"I think I look like I'm trying a little too hard to look like Hedy Lamarr,"* she humorously replied.

Above: Another star is born. Arlene Dahl in 1945. (Walter Thornton's collection)

More from that 1951 *Modern Screen* article:

"She went to Walter Thornton to get more introductions to theater people. 'I'll make you a top-flight model,' he said, 'but I can't introduce you to theater people.' He gave her $300 and sent her to Vogue magazine, where she started posing at $15.00 an hour. Within three months she was making $30.00 an hour ($505 according to the 2023 CPI). She appeared in Revlon ads and was the Edelbrau Beer Girl of 1946—but not an actress."

Ms. Dahl was cheerful and upbeat in her responses to us. *"Geez, it sounds like you want me to write the whole book myself,"* she jokingly cracked after one of our questions. She seemed to have given a lot of sincere thought to our email. Ms. Dahl told us that she signed with the Walter Thornton Agency because she had heard that his was more of a "boutique" agency than the others and offered more comprehensive, personalized representation than other New York agencies.

"He had me working full-time, every day, right away, and he fast-tracked my introduction to Diana Vreeland [fashion editor of Harper's Bazaar], which was what really set my career in motion," Arlene Dahl told us.

She instantly became a fixture on the pages of most of the glossy fashion magazines of the mid-1940s. She was Hollywood-ready. Her made-for-Technicolor red hair saw her soon whisked to "The Coast" where she signed a brief contract with Warner Brothers in 1947, to star opposite popular singing star Dennis Morgan in *My Wild Irish Rose.* A casting agent for MGM spotted her in the film and quickly signed her, after her Warner's contract was somehow allowed to lapse. MGM had her in mind as a triple-threat, musical comedy star, during what was the very peak of the MGM golden era of musicals. Within just a few years of modeling for the Walter Thornton Agency, she was given the full build-up by MGM as one of their brightest new stars.

We presume by reading notes and records our father saved relating to Arlene Dahl that she was something of a personal favorite of his. Her photo appeared in numerous Thornton Agency ads as their postwar Venus. By all accounts, she was a warm, kind, genuine person. She took her career very seriously, but she maintained a healthy sense of humor about her own outsized, ultra-glamorous image. She eventually became an expert on all things beauty-related, not unlike her former modeling agent. In 1952, she began writing a widely syndicated beauty advice column of her own. Two years later, she launched Arlene Dahl Enterprises, marketing her own line of cosmetics and deluxe lingerie. She wrote or contributed to numerous books on beauty-related topics, such as, *Always Ask a Man: Arlene Dahl's Key to Femininity*; *Arlene Dahl's Love Scopes* (she was a firm believer in astrology); and perhaps her best-known book, *Beyond Beauty.*

As we prepared to interview Ms. Dahl, I recalled a detached childhood memory related to Arlene Dahl. Dad was in his chair and I was on the sofa. She was appearing on a re-run of a television quiz show, like *Password*, or something like that. Probably in the late 1970s. When she was introduced by the host, our dad suddenly snapped to attention, saying. *"Well, would you look at her? She looks fantastic, and she's no youngster,"* he said. *"I always thought she was such a knockout. She was the real thing."* I remembered her name because I thought my dad said her name was "Doll," which I found kind of funny, a lady named "Doll," because I thought she actually looked like a doll. She was able to leverage her role as "Beauty Expert Arlene Dahl" for the rest of her life.

"As I said, he was at all times a perfect gentleman—the girls knew him as 'The Gentleman Agent,' strictly professional and widely respected," she concluded in her final email to us. *"And he was very good at what he did. My memories of him are all happy ones. You should be very proud of your father, since he was the best in the business,"* she kindly added.

We read the sad news of Arlene Dahl's passing just six months after we'd last made contact with her. We were so grateful to have communicated with her when we did. After learning about the number of other former Thornton Models who'd disavowed their modeling careers, to finally hear, first-hand, from just *one* of them, acknowledging our dad's contribution to their success was really gratifying. It's a fact that Ms. Dahl was the very last of the surviving Walter Thornton models who had successfully crossed over to Hollywood film stardom. She was it. We'll always be grateful to Arlene Dahl for remembering our dad so fondly. And from our dad's side, we're sure the feeling was mutual.

It's clear to us that Walter eventually accepted the inevitability that his "creations" would, of course, be desired in Hollywood. Rather than fight it, he learned to be a conduit for producers, directors and casting agents seeking to employ his models, on the other coast. Wisely, his agency contracts were fine-tuned with buyout clauses that went into effect once his models were tapped for Hollywood stardom. It's not hyperbole that we used his nickname the "Star Maker" in the title of this chapter, because the fact is, former Walter Thornton Agency models would go on to be nominated for acting Oscars twelve times-and five of them were Oscar winners.

Chapter 17

The Great Morale Booster

Nancy

"Victory has been pinned-up and fought for."— *Winifred Van Duzer*

During the course of our investigation, we frequently encountered references suggesting that our father was the originator of the pinup girl. Adriana expressed skepticism, asking, "*Could that be a mistake? I conducted research and found that the term 'pinup' had been used during the Spanish-American War and even the Civil War, when soldiers affixed illustrated depictions of women to their tents.*"

The persistent portrayal of our father as the Pin-Up King, credited with originating the pinup girl concept, both in various news stories and his personal advertising, prompted us to scrutinize this term more closely. To our revelation, the pinup girl wasn't attributed to a specific girl, but rather to a sweeping, enduring movement that bolstered the morale of World War II troops. Our father was the instigator of this movement, playing a substantial role in the wartime endeavor and leaving an invaluable legacy for us to unearth.

In the boxes, there were many typewritten pages with Dad's thoughts about the movement and one quote jumped out at us: "What's in a 'Pin-Up' that could stir the hearts of countless GI's, the curiosity of eminent professors, and the imagination of the public? There is more than meets the eye and for the Pin-Up story we go back to 1940." So we went back to when the movement started in 1940.

World War II was already taking place in Europe, and Roosevelt was preparing Americans for our inevitable inclusion. Even though the U.S. didn't officially enter the war until December 1941, its involvement was seen by most as an upcoming probability. To that end, in September 1940, the first peacetime draft was activated in the history of the country. Fort Dix, New Jersey was an induction center and training installation for thousands of draftees and was located only seventy-five miles south of Manhattan. As young men were being called to training, Walter naturally began to think back on his own training camp stint in the military during World War I.

He knew well the lonesome feeling that those soldiers would get as they would be away from their homes for long periods of time and many of them didn't see a feminine face or hear a feminine voice for months at a stretch. The majority of the soldiers, sailors, marines, fliers, and coast guardsmen were single, well below thirty and away from their homes for the very first time. The only diversion available to them was mail from their loved ones (which was quite irregular), camp shows or the occasional motion picture. And not all servicemen received letters. Often, in the more spartan environments, motion pictures, even if available, could not be shown. And as far as camp shows went, they were so infrequent that they were special events.

Walter thought about his days at the Columbus barracks, where he served. He didn't have anyone back home as he was homeless, missing companionship that had long been taken away. He observed how his fellow soldiers would pin sketches of beautiful women to their flimsy tent walls. Others clipped images from newspapers of film stars like Mary Pickford, "America's Sweetheart" and a key figure in patriotic propaganda. He'd been only fourteen years old, but he would mimic what the older guys were doing. He looked through whatever newspapers and magazines he could get, selected an image of a pretty girl, then clipped it and pinned it to his tent. Then one morning, after a night of storms, he awoke with frigid cold bed sheets. The rain on the canvas tent had drizzled through the small holes the pins had made. Adding insult to injury, he learned that pinning anything to the tents also happened to be against regulations, let alone impractical as hell. "*So there I and many others were with our beautiful companions, all soaking wet,*" he joked. At the time it was no laughing matter though, because he earned himself KP (kitchen police) duty for his trouble.

Now it was 1940 and Walter was no longer a kid in the army. This time he was Walter Thornton, head of the New York model agency bearing his name and internationally famous. He represented some of the most beautiful women on the planet. In this second war, soldiers were no longer in tents but in barracks with smooth walls on which you could tape or pin pictures.

It occurred to him that the boys in the army might find life more pleasant if they could look at the fresh feminine faces of some of the girls whose features graced the nation's magazine covers, billboards and advertisements. So, the notion came to him.... What if every soldier who wished to have real pictures of beautiful girls could have them just by asking, free of charge? A collection of pretty "Pin-Up Girls" to decorate their barracks. And, what's more, wouldn't it be nice if the pictures were personally autographed for him? Thornton sent a letter to General Powell, commander of Fort Dix, proposing to send an autographed copy of a favorite model to any serviceman desiring one, for free. General Powell called this gesture a welcome contribution to the aid of their morale in a letter dated December 16, 1940.

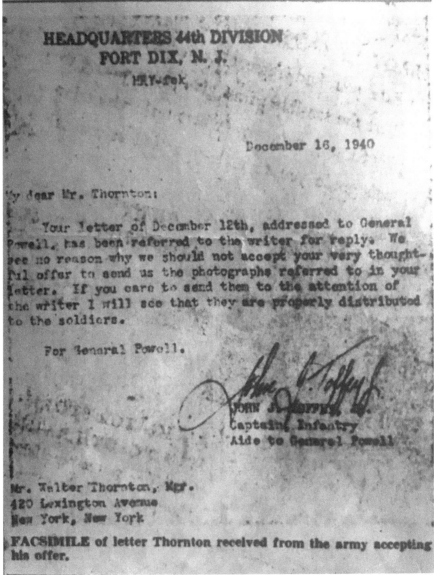

HEADQUARTERS 44th DIVISION
FORT DIX, N. J.

JJRY-fek

December 16, 1940

My dear Mr. Thornton:

Your letter of December 12th, addressed to General
Powell, has been referred to the writer for reply. We
see no reason why we should not accept your very thought-
ful offer to send us the photographs referred to in your
letter. If you care to send them to the attention of
the writer I will see that they are properly distributed
to the soldiers.

For General Powell.

JOHN J.
Captain, Infantry
Aide to General Powell

Mr. Walter Thornton, Mgr.
420 Lexington Avenue
New York, New York

FACSIMILE of letter Thornton received from the army accepting
his offer.

*Above: Walter Thornton offered to brighten the lives of conscripts at
Fort Dix by donating five thousand photographs of beautiful models to
decorate barracks. (New York Post, December 19, 1940)*

Walter dug out about five thousand photographs of his models and
the girls went to work autographing. He took them to Fort Dix. The
reaction was sensational and immediate. The donation of photos received wide publicity and in no time at all, his office was swamped

with letters and postcards from military installations and active-duty personnel all over the country clamoring for more. And not long after that, the requests started pouring in from overseas.

The Thornton Agency pledged one million photos for the troops, sent free of charge. Walter didn't just sit and wait for the requests to come in. He was proactive in informing all the boys at war that they could each have a photo or as many photos as they wanted. He advertised in major papers across the country and military post publications, promising a photo to any service member who wrote in with a request.

For the ones who had no sweethearts, girlfriends or wives, a "pinup girl" picture became the epitome of a wife, sweetheart or girlfriend. She was an impersonal but, at the same time, highly personal expression of "This is what we are fighting for." Nor were the women in service excluded from the offer. WACs, WAVEs, and other women serving overseas could request "handsome pin-up guys"—clean-cut, all-American boys—to boost their morale. Dad actively advertised for the recruitment of male models since many of his would-be models had gone to war. A promise was a promise and he had to find those all-American boys for the servicewomen.

And so, originated the legendary "pinup girl" of WWII. No longer was the term pinup girl used to describe how a soldier was displaying the images of women; it had transformed into a movement where mass-produced photographs of beautiful models were sent to servicemen. In turn, many of the models wound up becoming "pen pals" through their photographs with the servicemen/women via Dad's agency, giving them a friend back home to fight for. No one had done anything like that before for them.

Seeing the popularity of the pinup pictures sent by Walter Thornton, others followed his lead. Hollywood started distributing millions of pictures of glamorous stars beginning the following year, the most famous being the Betty Grable over-the-shoulder-glance shot which came along in 1943. The Thornton pinups mostly shied away from glamour in favor of the sweet and sexy girl next door—the girl any guy might have a chance to marry. Or, as one writer put it, "a refreshing 'typical American' type of girl, with sex appeal of course, but with clothes on—definitely."

Despite the rumors that servicemen would have preferred pictures of ladies of the night, the army heads, the psychologists and the folks back home were pleasantly surprised that the boys truly enjoyed the kind of pictures that were sent by Walter Thornton—the pictures of fresh, clean and decent girls that personified for the nation's fighting men the type of girl they used to date back home.

Adriana had pulled a file from Dad's boxes stuffed with many letters of thanks from actual service members. We didn't need any psychologist to make us understand why this idea was such a morale booster. Here's what some of them wrote:

"To Walter Thornton. Your Rita Daigle helped me get through my service in Guadalcanal. Her letters reminded me [of] everything I was fighting for. God bless you for sending her my way when I needed a friend the most because I have no family. Sincerely, Dave Haden, Harrisburg, Penna." [1946]

"To the Pin-Up King, You are the king in my book. I made it through the war and so did my pinups. Thank you for making our ship look a lot prettier. Me and all the guys in my unit all had our pinups, but I think mine was the prettiest, Myra Keck. Thank you. Stanley Kellso, St. Cloud, Minnesota" [1945].

"Pin-ups restore my faith in humanity"

"Each night, after a back-breaking day and no mail, I look at your picture, and then I smile, and feel that I have good reason to keep fighting. For you are my Dream Girl."

"You can't begin to realize what it means to a guy who has been overseas for two years to get a picture of a real, honest-to-goodness American girl, particularly one as lovely as your-self. No serviceman appreciates the American girl until he tries to find her equal anywhere else."

"As did thousands of others, I came into the service without a girl-friend. It's such a good feeling to know that some girl is thinking about you part of the time."

"A girl's photo is the best friend any fellow away from home could possibly have."

Other letters had requests for the models to meet up with them when the soldier came home, and in fact sometimes the models did meet soldiers at home on furlough or in hospitals. One model laughed that she received seven marriage proposals in a single night. Another model ended up marrying an officer who had once known her as his favorite pinup girl. Other letters were more serious: One pinup girl received a half-burned photo from a GI—along with a note saying it had stopped a piece of shrapnel and saved his life.

Throughout the war, Walter continued to send thousands of pictures, personally autographed by his models, without cost, to all parts of the world and to every G.I. who asked for one. Camp and unit service publications who regularly featured the Thornton pinups in their pages reported them as top circulation boosters. An editor of *Army Weekly* stated, "Our readers are demanding more Thornton pin-up pictures." Later the pinup photos were found in jeeps, tanks, and planes, in fox-holes, and in hospital wards.

From Dad's writings:

*"More than 2 million pictures (*he was still sending them in 1949), *each of which bore the legend, "A Walter Thornton Model," were sent to G.I.s in the United States, Europe, Asia, the Philippines, the Aleutians and even more remote parts of the world."* Dad employed over sixty models to keep up with the demand. *"The Pin-Up Girl by Thornton is an American Tradition,"* Walter wrote, *"and in the fervor of wartime and postwar patriotism, everybody wanted to be a pin-up girl—or to associate their products with her."* With so much enthusiasm about his pinups, Water decided to protect his huge investment and got insurance for his top models to the tune of $10,000 each ($217,000 according to the 2023 CPI). According to the Associated Press in 1940, this was the first time in history that photographic models were given insurance protection.

Above: (L to R) Models Jeanine Saunders, Peggy Diggins and Frances Garriet receiving insurance policies from Walter Thornton. February 1, 1940.

Several pinup girls were approached by Hollywood agents, including his insured top models like Peggy Diggins and Pat Vaniver (Dolores Donlon), who both later became film actresses. Beauty experts gave advice on how to take a picture like a pinup girl. *American Notes and Queries,* a respected academic periodical, sent an inquiry to Walter

Thornton as to the origin of the words "pinup girl". His insights were published in its May 1946 issue and have been quoted as part of history in other publications (*"War Slang, American Fighting Words and Phrases Since The Civil War"* and others). H.L. Mencken, (1880-1956) an American journalist and expert in American English, who is famous for his work *"The American Language"* (a big study about how Americans speak English), also attributes the "Pinup Girl" to our father (*Carnal Knowledge: Baxter's Concise Encyclopedia of Modern Sex" in 2009*).

Once again, our father saw something no one else had seen and jumped ahead of the pack, to create something new.

Chapter 18

The "Pin-Up King" Empire

Adriana

The 1940s had been a stage of meaningful activity in our father's full life. However, it wasn't until we delved into a comprehensive investigation that we came to appreciate the significance of this phase in his life. It was a time period ripe with important endeavors spanning the wartime years and beyond, principally starting with the pinup girl movement.

The once-familiar moniker of "Merchant of Venus" that had been associated with Dad was undergoing a transformation, evolving into "The Pin-Up King," while his models became widely recognized as "Pin-Up Girls." In parallel, John Robert Powers' models were renowned as Powers Girls, and the newly arrived Harry Conover models were referred to as Cover Girls.

Shortly after the launch of the pinup girl movement Walter embarked on designing exclusive swimsuits tailored for his pinup girls in 1942. These initial creations showcased the sensibility of wartime ingenuity given the shortage in supplies by using scarves, men's handkerchiefs, and souvenir parachutes. Each swimsuit was adorned with a distinctive brass safety pin, identifying the model as a Walter Thornton pinup girl.

Subsequently, as returning GIs implored their partners to acquire swimsuits like those worn by the pinup girls, letters flooded Walter's agency. In answer, Walter licensed his designs to a knitwear company, thereby making them accessible to the general public.

A pivotal milestone arrived in 1944 when our father officially solid-
ified the exclusive usage of "Walter Thornton Pin-Up Girl" by trade-
marking it. This trademark extended beyond swimsuits, encompassing
a diverse range of licensed merchandise such as hat boxes, handbags,
and travel bags, cementing his legacy in a multifaceted manner.

WALTER THORNTON
PIN-UPS

Above: Walter Thornton pin-up models in bathing suits, 1940s

Many of his top models achieved recognition as winners in beauty
contests, such as Miss Stardust or Miss Rheingold, where countless

young women competed for these prestigious titles. Walter entered into partnerships with the organizers of these contests, extending modeling contracts to the winners. His influence also extended to the judging process, allowing him a role in helping to select the winners. Notably, he even entered some of his own models into these competitions, a strategic move aimed at showcasing their exceptional qualities.

Once his triumphant models were established, a grand-scale promotional campaign was set in motion—an endeavor of truly remarkable proportions. We saw a headline from the August 1945 edition of the *New York Post* that said, "World's Largest Pin-Up Picture Unveiled Today." The article continued to say that ten famous pinup models from the Thornton Agency showed up at Palisades Amusement Park, each showing their impressive life-sized, six-foot-tall pinup pictures. These amazing women met with soldiers in real life, gave them signed photos, and made a strong bond. Walter himself was at the event, saying hello and honoring the military attendees.

"We believed the life-sized photos to be the largest pinup pictures in the world, until we uncovered one towering like a sixteen-foot-tall billboard!" The subject of this colossal distinction was Eleanor Cahill of Coronado, California. Her selection was propelled by her recent triumph as the winner of the Miss Stardust contest, a title gained from a pool of over eight thousand contestants across the nation. Stardust, a prominent lingerie manufacturer in New York, hosted these widely anticipated contests that drew participants in droves. Cahill's victory was rewarded with a five-hundred-dollar war bond and national exposure. Rita Daigle had previously claimed the title of Miss Stardust in 1944, further solidifying her status as one of Dad's most highly compensated models, eventually securing a contract with Paramount Pictures.

Eleanor Cahill began modeling for Dad's agency at the age of 17, after she and two friends applied to become models. Successfully making the cut, she embarked on a three-year journey as a prominent model for Dad's agency. In 2019, we made contact with Eleanor's daughter, who shared the bittersweet news that her mother was transitioning to a memory care facility. In a heartfelt gesture, Eleanor's daughter unveiled a treasure trove of memories encapsulated within her mother's "memory box," a collection replete with photographs chronicling her vibrant life as a cherished Walter Thornton pinup girl. While individuals like Mrs. Cahill and many of Dad's pinup models may not have achieved the level of fame associated with pinup movie stars like Betty Grable, it was evident from numerous news articles that Walter Thornton's pinups held great appeal among countless soldiers.

Beyond their role as pinup models, these young women played many roles in patriotic initiatives. They showcased the emerging war-approved fashion trends, sporting slimmer, tapered silhouettes that conserved fabric. Engaging smiles adorned photographs that depicted their involvement in scrap drives and victory gardens. Their contributions extended to boosting troop morale during farewells and spearheading war bond rallies. In one such instance, those who invested significantly in bonds were rewarded with a special treat—a date with one of the pinup girls. They performed all these activities in addition to their dedicated autographing and sending photos with uplifting messages to soldiers in need of encouragement. We marveled at astonishing images that captured the soldiers, post-pinup events, carrying away life-sized renditions of the pinups.

A particular discovery filled us with joy: 'The World's Largest Pin-Up' featuring Eleanor Cahill was entrusted to sail the Pacific waters, proudly adorning the U.S.S. Missouri battleship—a fitting tribute to a remarkable era and the enduring legacy of these captivating pinup girls.

Above: October 1945 19-year-old Eleanor Cahill of Coronado, CA., with "The World's Largest Pin-up": a photo that measured sixteen feet tall. (Walter Thornton archives)

Could Walter top his previous accomplishments? Absolutely. In 1945, he unveiled another remarkable endeavor—bringing his pinups to life. Amidst a Navy gathering at Palisades Park, the Thornton Agency orchestrated a captivating spectacle: a newsreel capturing the transition of real-life models from their life-sized photographs into three-dimensional reality. This mesmerizing spectacle was subsequently showcased in theaters across the nation. Fortunately, we stumbled upon one such reel, providing us the opportunity to witness firsthand the enchanting transformation.

With a sense of wonder, we observed as these graceful models tore through the photographs, breaching the barrier between the two-dimensional image and real live girl.

Above: Newspaper advertisement (Daily News, June 26, 1946)

Yet, the ingenuity behind Walter's pinup movement continued to unveil fresh ideas full of creativity. We found a *New York Daily News* article dated February 1, 1948, chronicling Dad's collaboration with a retail display manufacturer, giving rise to store mannequins inspired by his most revered pinup models. A departure from the norm, these mannequins transcended the conventional portrayal of mere clothing showcases, encapsulating the very essence of the pinup ideals.

Traditionally confined to partial forms and lacking distinct features, mannequins had heretofore been faceless canvases for garments. However, with an innovative vision, a multidisciplinary team united models, makeup artists, and sculptors, synergizing their talents to craft lifelike mannequins. Every detail was meticulously considered, from the texture of their hair and the hues of their eyes, down to precise measurements and the characteristics that rendered each model's expression unique. Walter, who once dreamed of becoming a sculptor, was now channeling his creativity into sculpting an array of exquisite model women to perfection.

The resulting mannequins, bearing the unmistakable looks of the Walter Thornton pinups such as Gloria Whalen, Rita Daigle, and Vicki Hazel graced display windows across the nation. As consumers, including the returning war veterans, strolled past these showcases, they were met with familiar pinup icons. Walter's endeavor had seamlessly brought his cherished pinup girls into the hearts of those who strolled the bustling streets.

Above: (L) Model Vicki Hazel, Gloria Whalen and Rita Daigle with their respective mannequins' replicas with Walter Thornton inspecting them (R) Model Vicki Hazel with her mannequin replica Below: (L) Model Gloria Whalen with Walter Thornton getting facial measurements (R) Model Rita Daigle with her mannequin replica (Star Tribune Minneapolis, Minnesota February 1, 1948)

This was all glamorous and amazing, but behind the scenes, there was a lot of hard work and expense involved. The backdrop of a world embroiled in war lent an additional layer of complexity. I stumbled upon a letter, a window into the past, where Dad corresponded with a *Glamour* magazine publisher in 1946. He penned, *"Much was the cost of grooming, promoting, and advertising the pin-up girl, including the distribution of her photographs gratis, well over a million copies that were sent to GIs throughout the world, have amounted to hundreds of thousands of dollars."* Remarkably, even then, Dad's dedication knew no bounds; his commitment persisted until the majority of servicemen had safely returned home.

Nancy and I came to realize that Dad's unwavering commitment to the pinup movement spanned over a decade.

Nancy jokingly asked, *"Is that where all of our inheritance went?"*

I giggled and replied, *"Y*es! *I think he ended up sending over two million copies! We could have been wealthy, but it's heartening to know that Dad laid the foundation for such a patriotic movement!"*

"Did you know it took Dad three years to produce the newsreel of the pinup girls bursting through their posters?" Nancy said. She pointed to a letter from Dad to *News of the Day* dated June 4, 1947, which which explained the protracted timeline.

The journey began in 1943, a year marked by the preparation and assembly of several dozen six-foot blow-ups. Multiples of each girl were crafted, anticipating potential retakes if the 'burst-through' sequences didn't align flawlessly. However, the tumultuous events of that year, including the Allied invasion of mainland Europe, temporarily shelved the project. Another surge of effort ensued in 1945, leading to the creation of new, more spectacular blow-up images. Alas, the project faced yet another halt, this time due to the seismic news of the atomic bomb and the subsequent end of the war.

With the war's conclusion, and despite myriad obstacles including postponements and adverse weather, the production was reignited, featuring Walter's latest bevy of stunning models. The persistence paid off on June 13, 1946, when the captivating vision of pinup girls stepping through their life-sized portraits at Palisades Park materialized.

Dad's resolute spirit endured throughout his life. When he set his sights on a goal, he channeled unwavering effort into its realization, ensuring it was done thoroughly and impeccably. An exception was his dream of the tile house in Ajijic. We believe that the house achieved completion upon his passing, as that was when work on the house stopped. Yet, his yearning to build individual bungalows for each of his six beloved children remained unrealized, a vision prevented by external circumstances. Dad was happy in the company of his family and envisioned a haven for them nearby. Regrettably, only two bungalows materialized, as the adjacent lot's owners withheld their decision to sell until after his death.

Chapter 19

A Tribute to Walter Thornton

Nancy

W hat is a great story without musical accompaniment? Our dad would tell you it's imperative. And Walter Thornton had musical accompaniment in not one, but three songs written about him. "*This is pretty crazy,*" I said, pulling a file containing three separate copies of sheet music that had been paper-clipped together. The intervening years in the damp, tropical climate of Ajijic had completely rusted the large paper clip that held them together, staining the yellowed music straight through. Walter Thornton was on the cover of all three songs, whose titles were, "Get a Pin-Up Girl," "The Walter Thornton Rhumba" and "The Pin-Up Polka," all three from 1946-47.

Above: Promotional photos of the song "Get A PIN-UP Girl" and a record (Walter Thornton archives)

"Aren't these the songs we used to play on the old, wind-up record player when we were little?" I asked. *"Remember how we used to think it sounded like the singers were singing 'Walter Thornton'? Well, looks like they were!"*

Navy chief officer Donald Wolf, stationed in the South Pacific, was so taken with Walter's pinup photos that he penned a song—"Get a Pin-Up Girl"—and dedicated it to Walter Thornton, the "Model King." The lyrics echo the feelings of servicemembers overseas:

"If your paper doll is torn,
And her edges slightly worn,

Boy, do you need Walter Thornton,
Get a Pin-Up Girl!"

Sam Donahue, once the Navy band leader, first introduced the song to the airwaves and set it on its way to becoming the newest big hit. It was subsequently recorded by one of the most popular radio personalities of the time, Jerry Cooper, accompanied by several Thornton pinups on background vocals. Walter threw his promotional efforts behind the song, offering it free to DJs on request; daily radio programs also chose "Get a Pin-Up Girl" as their theme song, given its popularity. We came across dozens of photographs of dad, and the pinup girls, with disc jockeys from all over the USA promoting the songs. They were frequently featured on the covers of popular music magazines like *Billboard* and *Cashbox*. Like we said, when dad had something in mind, he went all out to make it a success.

The Pin-Up King became an almost folkloric figure to servicemen at home and abroad. Without argument, from a publicity standpoint, Walter had leapt to the head of the modeling pantheon during the WWII years. His reputation in the United States as an all-purpose, beauty powerhouse seemed to double with each passing year, with no end in sight.

Above: The anteroom of the Thornton Agency's office in the Graybar Building, 1945. The Pin-Up King welcomes decommissioned service-men back from overseas, including future film noir star, Bill Williams (second from left), whom the Thornton Agency would represent after the war.

On the heels of the "Get a Pin-Up Girl' success, there came more pinup hits. *"Pin-up girls, pin-up girls, they make men go WOOF WOOF WOOF!"* Adriana sang while reading the lyrics to "The Pin-Up Polka." *"Remember how we used to sing this one?"* We later researched the writers of "Walter Thornton Rhumba" and "The Pin-Up Polka." They were Albert Gamse and Irving Fields, a venerable Tin Pan Alley song-writing team who enjoyed rhumba-craze success in the mid-twentieth century. They had previously collaborated on the popular songs "Man-agua Nicaragua" and "Miami Beach Rhumba". Separately, Gamse's most personal success was being tapped to write the official lyrics to the U.S. presidential anthem, "Hail to the Chief." We find it pretty amusing that the same man who wrote, *"Hail to the Chief, as we pledge cooperation,"* also wrote, *"Pin-up girls, pin-up girls, they make men go WOOF WOOF WOOF!"* The lyrics of "Pin-Up Polka" also state:

"If you haven't got a pin-up
Keep your chin up,
While I ring Mr. Walter Thornton,
For he's the Pin-Up King..."

Seeing this sheet music took me right back to our childhood, and how my three young sisters and two brothers and I liked to stage little musical numbers for our parents. We'd even create a makeshift stage on the courtyard terrace of the castle. And we would play the seventy-eight RPM records our dad kept in a suitcase—on an old-fashioned, table-top, wind-up Victrola that required no electricity and seemed almost magical to us. The fact that our father's name, "Walter Thornton" appeared in several of the records' titles and lyrics never gave us particular pause. It was another entry for the "too strange to comprehend" file. We'd played those records countless times—probably hundreds—and it never properly registered with any of us that these songs were actually about *our* Walter Thornton. The Walter Thornton Rhumba recording we had was on a London label with the well-known Cuban-styled bandleader/vocalist Edmundo Ros singing:

It's good news I bring,
'Bout Walter Thornton, the 'Pin-Up King,'
He left his native Manhattan,
To pick some pin-ups á la Latin....

How prescient these lyrics are, considering it was written in 1947, eleven years before Dad moved to Mexico and met our mother. The song was also recorded by Jose Morand (Victor Label), Don Pablo (Rondo label), and Noro Morales (also known as the Rhumba King-MGM label). The song was judged in one review as having "punch and character."

Sitting down decades later to read the sheet music lyrics of the three known songs that were written either about, or in tribute to, our father, we were rather amazed at our previous inability to make the connection: They were singing about our dad.

"They say his full name <u>eleven times</u>! How did we never get that?"
Adriana asked me.

As for the plain-as-day, multiple mentions of our father in the lyrics, if it was in any way processed by us, it was more along the lines of, "*The guy they're singing about has the same name as Papi!*" The final chorus features Edmundo Ros and chorus all chanting to a pulsating, rhumba beat:

Chorus*: WALTER THORNTON!*

Soloist*: Olé, olé, olé*

Chorus*: WALTER THORNTON!*

Soloist: *Please pin me up with a girl today,*

Chorus*: WALTER THORNTON!*

Soloist & Chorus: *Olé, olé, olé, olé*

When we'd sing along, we would actually sing "Walter Thornton," as if we were the ones being clever and inserting our dad's name into the song. And he never once revealed himself as the very "Pin-Up King" they refer to in the lyrics. Just imagine if your own businessman father was actually being sung about ...on a record. Too absurd to even consider, right? At least it was to us.

It's a pretty catchy tune, especially if you're into rhumbas. Far superior, we think, to "The Humphrey Bogart Rhumba," or even "The Walter Winchell Rhumba"; each of those men had their own rhumbas, too, during the "Rhumba Craze" of the 1930s to the 1950s. Nearly all the major nightclub venues in New York and Hollywood had their own, in-residence rhumba bands. The in-house rhumba band at the Stork Club had "The Walter Thornton Rhumba" in its repertoire, because Walter was known to visit there frequently in the postwar years. It may seem frivolous today, but to have a rhumba named in one's honor was quite something during that era. It became sort of a swanky calling card. When someone with an eponymous rhumba entered a nightclub in New York, in, say, 1948, the band conductor was known to switch tunes, even in the midst of another song, in order to herald the dignitary's arrival, whose entrance was then often greeted by applause. Having a personal theme song was something of a societal badge of honor, and our father had three of them; tunes that would travel with him wherever he went, announcing his arrival. Look who's here!

Chapter 20

The Pinup Room

Adriana

T he pinup photos, booklets, calendars, bathing suits, songs, contests, newsreels, mannequins, personal appearances, and any other various outcroppings of the Walter Thornton pinup mania weren't quite enough. Not yet. In 1946, that immediate postwar year of prosperity, Walter Thornton opened an intimate and chic supper club, the Pin-Up Room, with a small group of partners, the walls of which were decorated with his pinup photographs in life size. It was a welcoming place where servicemen could dine next to their favorite pinup pictures—and on some occasions they'd be lucky enough to dine next to the real model herself!

The main room and bar of the restaurant were lined with pictures of fourteen of his most popular pinup beauties. Mounted on chartreuse feather-edged sheets of paper, against celadon-green walls, the pictures appeared to be pages ripped from a giant book. To carry out the pinup motif, large ornamental pins were placed in the corner of each picture. In an adjoining room, the rose-tinted walls carried on the pinup theme with smaller photos.

Walter was the front man for the Pin-Up Room, his latest offshoot business venture under the ever-expanding umbrella of Walter Thornton, Inc. The instant success of the New York supper club spurred the group to look into taking their idea worldwide, hoping to expand it to an elite chain of Pin-Up Rooms across the globe, with Honolulu mentioned as the locale for Pin-Up Room number two. The actual nuts-and-bolts, daily operation of the club was not in Walter's wheelhouse—he'd leave that to the pros. His roles as "Merchant of Venus" and "Pin-Up King" were his contribution to the enterprise. He and his luxury brand gave the club its theme.

TONI EDEN

Above: A Toni Eden pinup, as seen on the walls of the Pin-Up Room, 1946

Thornton Models included in the Pin-Up Room were: Patricia Vaniver (Dolores Donlon), Gloria Whalen, Rita Daigle, Silvia MacNell, Mattie Reid, Yvonne Lewis, Eleanor Cahill, Jackey Kendricks, Betty Anne Creegan, Betty Ardell, Mary Evans and you could hardly miss the larger-than-life-sized, pinup poster of Walter Thornton's newest model, Toni Eden. When you entered the intimate nightclub there she was, facing the entrance right behind the piano.

She had only recently started going by the name of Toni Eden, having been rechristened by her agent. Previously, she had been known by her real name, Walda Winchell, and she was the daughter of Walter Winchell. The Thornton Agency took on Walda as one of its most prominent Walter Thornton pinup models. Our father would have been the first to deny any quid pro quo favoritism, despite Winchell's many positive column mentions over the years.

The Thornton Agency's exacting standards of beauty were something it couldn't afford to gamble on by hiring a sub-par model as a "favor," even if the favor was to benefit the most powerful show-business figure in America. Walter actually found Walda's luxuriant, russet hair and flashing blue eyes to be quite striking. Walter sincerely saw potential in his newest Thornton model.

W alter Thornton's in-person appearances at the Pin-Up Room were timed and choreographed for maximum dramatic impact. When he'd enter the club, the in-house cocktail pianist, Charles Strouse, would rip right into a jazzy, up-tempo rendition of "Get a Pin-Up Girl" to indicate the arrival of the Pin-Up King, himself. Eager G.I.s returning to New York City from overseas made Walter's nightspot a must-see destination, hoping to actually meet their pinup dream girls in the flesh.

The club stood roughly equidistant between Grand Central and Pennsylvania Stations, a corridor that was already flush with returning soldiers and sailors who were, at long last, on American shores again. As such, the location of the Pin-Up Room was chosen with maximum G.I. visibility in mind: the northwest corner of East 34th Street and Lexington Avenue, in the shadow of The Chrysler Building.

The Pin-Up Room had been an instant hit when it had its grand opening in 1946, the latest entry into the "Manhattan-Merry-Go-Round", as the glittering nightclub circuit of New York was called in those post-war boom years. We're especially proud of another element that set the Pin-Up Room apart from many of the other swanky nightlife offerings of the day. While it wasn't unheard of in the early 1950s, it was certainly an exception for black performers to headline in New York cabarets.

I can't help but think that even though our dad wouldn't have necessarily been responsible for booking the headline performers at his Pin-Up Room, as the de facto head of the club, he would certainly have been part of the chain of approval that encouraged the club to be a desegregated one, both onstage and off.

The Pin-Up Room proudly presented Miss Mabel Mercer. At that point in her career, Mabel Mercer had developed a following of devotees, who found her skill with delivering lyrics to be transportive. In truth, she was equal parts vocalist and storyteller. It was her evocative phrasing that really set her apart from other singers. Returning African American G.I.s were heartily welcomed home at the Pin-Up Room. That was hardly the norm at the time, either.

The heyday of the Pin-Up Room ran side by side with the popularity of the legendary Stork Club. But the racially welcoming tone of the Pin-Up Room served as a reverse image of the larger, and *strictly* segregated, Stork Club. Mabel Mercer was presented as a precious gem by the Pin-Up Room. Just her, beneath a solo spot, seated in an armchair, next to a piano, weaving her magic spell on the audience.

Frank Sinatra was known to frequent the Pin-Up Room whenever Mabel Mercer was performing there. More than just an ardent fan, Sinatra had completely lost his voice for several months and later gave credit for his vocal recovery to studying the technique of Mabel Mercer. For almost a decade, Walter Thornton dedicated his energies to promoting the overall pinup girl movement.

Among our findings is a letter dated June 14, 1946, authored by our father and addressed to Mr. M.D. Clofine of *News of the Day*. Within this correspondence, he articulated: "So favorable the impression and the good-will it established in the public eye, that it was well worth those years of growth coupled with mounting costs." And indeed, since Walter's time, the pinup girl notion has evolved, but remains nonetheless an American tradition.

Chapter 21

A Setback

Nancy

Adriana and I hadn't really delved into our dad's 1950s period yet. We'd learned almost nothing about that decade yet, and it was time.

I drove the twenty or so miles from my home to the main Dallas Public Library. Through the years, I'd spent countless hours and days in various libraries, especially during my time in law school, as well as in my eventual capacity as an attorney. So intensive study and research were always a large part of my job. In other words, I knew my way around a microfiche machine.

Microfiche research is a fairly labor-intensive procedure, which involves slowly, manually feeding photographic film rolls into an imposing-looking projector, by hand, and advancing/reversing it with a little hand crank—though it did have electronic fast-forward/rewind buttons. And everything is in negative resolution: black page, white print.

I'd brought ten rolls of nickels, having been told in advance that Xerox copies were five cents apiece—and I was hoping I'd need a lot of nickels. In those pre-online newspaper archive days, I wanted to see what I could find out about the 1950s' version of The Merchant of Venus. I truly had no idea of what I was about to discover.

The microfiche reels in the bin that the librarian had selected for me had all been flagged as connected to Walter Thornton. Nearly all of them were from 1954. The first reel the librarian's assistant had loaded for me contained the contents of the *New York Daily News*—January-February 1954. I started by scanning through the first twenty-five days of January. As I zipped through the sports pages at the end of that edition, past the large photo of Marilyn Monroe and Joe DiMaggio honeymooning in Korea, I accidentally scanned past the front page of the following day's edition (January 26, 1954). But even in fast-forward mode, white-against-black, the day's banner headline could hardly have escaped my notice:

I actually gasped aloud and jumped as I quickly spooled backwards. Thornton wasn't an uncommon name. *"Must be some other Thornton,"* I thought. Story on Page 3...scroll down...

Thornton Arrested in 600G Kid Model Gyp

By Gerald Kessler and Neal Patterson

Walter Thornton, models' agent who publicized himself as "The Merchant of Venus," was arrested at 3 P. M. yesterday and accused of heading a $600,000 photo racket preying largely on fond parents eager to see their youngsters strike it rich in modeling or TV.

Queens authorities charged that "hundreds" of complaints of misrepresentation had been made against Thornton. They added that numbers of top names in Hollywood and TV

NEWS ON THE AIR
TELEVISION—WNBC—Channel 11

RADIO—WABC—Dial 1130

eeling Fine;
has Prove It

—including Lauren Bacall, Marilyn Monroe, Joan Crawford, Dorothy McGuire and Shelley Winters—have denied claims that Thornton was instrumental in their success.

(NEWS foto by Art Edger)
Walter Thornton (left) is booked by Detective Edward Murtaugh.

Above: (L) The January 25, 1954 front page of the New York Daily News, as seen on negative image microfilm (R) Walter Thornton's hands are somewhat hidden behind mesh fencing in front of the Queen's men's detention center—to the probable regret of the mob of press photographers it was staged for—obscuring the fact that he was being led away handcuffed. But he was smiling.

It was so utterly shocking and confusing I found my eyes were involuntarily welling up with tears. I somehow made it through most of the article. And though I tried to keep it together, I suddenly started sobbing. My vocal outburst resonated throughout the large, open research hall. I had a vague realization that everyone was staring at me, as if I were the first person they'd ever witnessed shrieking at microfiche.

The nice lady who'd greeted me at the entrance desk ran over to me and softly placed her hand on my shoulder, asking, *"Are you all right, honey?"* I simply pointed to the close-up, reverse-image picture of my smiling father and wailed some more. I could even detect his smile in reverse-image. Seeing him smiling—while under arrest—was just too much for me. The librarian helped me gather my belongings, and even proactively retrieved my coat and my bag from the checkroom for me. She seemed to realize it was a prudent move for me to wrap up this research trip and get out of her library as fast as possible.

I left with all my nickels still in their rolls, without a single photocopy. I didn't ever want to see those headlines again. The Texas skies chose to open up and pour, just as I was leaving. Unfortunately, my umbrella was in the car three blocks away. I dove into my car, thoroughly drenched, gripping the wheel and trying to process what I'd just learned about our dad. I was filled with confusion and revulsion. My heart was pounding.

What am I going to tell my family?

The first one I messaged, of course, was my sister. I sent her a carefully worded email about what I had just discovered. I wanted to try to make it sound not too terrible. But it *was* terrible! From what I'd just read, the accusations against our father were stunningly harsh. Grand theft? Criminal fraud? Racketeering? Those were the words that leapt out at me from that 1954 front-page article. And those words were being used to describe my Papi. In bold, triple-point headlines.

The article said that he had been under FBI surveillance. The district attorney of Queens, New York said that our father had been a miscreant all his life. One tabloid writer even called him a "dead-end kid...born in a log cabin."

"*Wow, I just read your email,*" Adriana said, calling me on my landline. "*That's really shocking. I need to see that for myself.*" She then asked, "*Did you get copies of the articles?*"

"*I didn't even think about making copies of any of it,*" I said. "*It was all so ugly and horrible. I just wanted to get out of there.*"

"*Do you at least remember the dates on the microfiche?*" Adriana asked.

"*Yes, January to June, 1954. He was arrested on January 25, 1954,*" I said.

"*So, he was actually arrested? Like, 'put-in-jail' arrested?*" she asked.

"*Yes, and not just him, ten of his female employees were arrested, too, in something called a 'child model racket,'*" I said.

"*I need to see what I can find on the internet about this,*" Adriana said.

"*I know this will probably sound lame, after all the work we've put into this,*" I said, "*but this has really stopped me in my tracks.*" I went on, "*I've already decided I've learned enough about Papi. If there is anything really bad, I don't want to know it.*" As I said these words, I tried to convince myself I really believed them—that I honestly did not wish to learn any more about what happened to our father. How on earth did everything fall apart so drastically?

"I see what you mean. Like, what if we were to discover something really terrible about him," Adriana asked, *"would that somehow cancel out all our good memories of him?"*

"That's exactly what I mean. It makes me afraid. It's too risky," I said. *"We could be opening a Pandora's Box here. Is it possible he never talked about his life before Mexico for just this reason?"*

So, just like that, we called off our research project—for several years, in fact. It tormented both Adriana and me, suddenly shutting down this channel toward learning who our father had been. It was really conflicting—and looking back, it was also really insincere and, frankly, cowardly. Being frozen in place by fearing the unknown was definitely not something that would have been espoused by our dad—or by his mentor, Dale Carnegie.

Nonetheless, that remained our status quo for almost a decade. We simply stopped all research and tried to focus on other things. Just as our mother had, we chose to focus not on the past but on the present. We had five kids and two husbands between us who needed our attention. We all had our framed *Seabiscuit* photos and other photos of him hanging in our homes to keep our dad's memory present in our daily lives. We spent all those years naively thinking our research was over—when, in fact, our real research had only just begun.

Chapter 22

Storm Clouds

Adriana

A round 2015, we slowly found ourselves almost involuntarily dip-ping back into our deep dive into our father's former life. Even-tually, we dove fully back into it after coming to the realization we just needed to know the truth—and that nothing we could find out about our father could affect how we felt about him—no matter what. So, we launched our search once again by digging into the post-WWII years, to find out how things had gone so terribly off course.

By 1950, Walter's new business cards read: "Walter Thornton, Pub-lisher." He'd taken his modeling agency to the very top—but he felt he'd "done it" and had other avenues he wished to explore. He was eliminating several of his business ventures and wanted to take a far less active role in the daily operation of his corporation. Walter was seeking a role wherein he could conduct his daily affairs from his home office at his 5 Tudor Place penthouse. Winding down so suddenly didn't really seem like him, but it all became clear when we discovered that Walter had suffered from debilitating back pain most of his adult life.

We knew Dad's back pain was one of the main motivating factors in his move to Ajijic. Here he would be closer to the thermal waters in the nearby town of San Juan Cosala. He also had the base of his bed made of cement to make it as firm as possible since that was what his doctors had recommended at the time. He had various other treatments for his pain as far back as any of us could remember. But what we were to find out was that his back pain had started long before; as early as the late

1930s. Though as a younger man he had been able to manage it, age caught up with him and brought pain so intense he underwent surgery for it in 1946. The operation helped, but only temporarily.

Our father's 1946 television series, *The Thornton Show*, was not renewed after its initial, twenty-six-week contract with CBS ran out—much to the relief of Mr. and Mrs. Walter Thornton, who had rather panicked upon realizing the massive investment of time, energy and money that a weekly, live television show entailed at a time when he was recovering from major back surgery. So in the immediate years that followed, Walter's main focus remained on his true vocation: that of representing and promoting his stable of some of the greatest beauties of the era. And his pinup enterprises were still very much in motion. His Pin-Up Room remained as popular as ever.

Unfortunately, with the return of his back pain he knew he could no longer effectively be an active agent. He even turned down an offer from a movie studio in 1947 for the making of a pinup girl film. Regarding the return of his back pain, Judy said in an affidavit: "I recall that he would often take treatments several times a week to ease the pain. From 1949 until the time that we were divorced and during the period I lived with him I can recall that he always was in a great deal of pain." It was a contributing factor to their marriage having fallen into severe disrepair. They were separated in 1950, for one year, and finally divorced in 1954.

Judy did note that the pain affected his temper, and a former employee shed a more detailed light on what his physical condition had done to his successful career. "He suffered intense pain from a back condition," she wrote in a statement, "that impaired his ability to conduct his business affairs. At the time that I left his employment [1950], he had become impossible to work for because of his irritability and nervousness caused by the pain. On many occasions he would not come to the office for days, and, when he did come to the office, he would often remain doubled up in pain and refuse to see anyone." Despite his outward success, he was really struggling.

He decided to reshape Walter Thornton, Inc., by leading it in yet another direction. He had been opening a series of offices and modeling schools in various cities that would continue under their respective managements. They would not be a time drain; he would only need to keep an advisory eye on them. So his main operation would be centered around modeling catalogs, just like before—but this time, for children and babies only. He hadn't landed upon this new concept coincidentally. It was only the latest in a career-long pattern of his being able to spot the trend—and be there to meet it.

With the ending of WWII, he knew that his concept of the Walter Thornton pinup girls would need to undergo some major rethinking, since his key demographic, military men, were now returning to America and a vast percentage of them were marrying and having children. And, in the postwar years, America couldn't seem to get enough of seeing children and babies in advertising.

Over 4,000
Walter Thornton
CHILDREN'S PICTURES to choose from
Three Volumes of Children's Pictures —
Every Model Hand-Picked by Walter Thornton

Survey after survey tells the same story. Children's pictures attract more attention in advertising than any other type of illustration — and that includes newspaper and magazine ads, counter and window displays, billboards, and direct mail!

And to put more attention-value into your ads, here's your chance to own and use the most complete, up-to-the-minute collection of child model pictures ever published — three big volumes of juvenile photos — all ages and types!

By the end of the war, Thornton child models were showing up in countless magazines, newspapers, circular ads, calendars, and mail order catalogs. And so the time was ripe to focus his energies on expanding that segment of his business. As he said to an interviewer, *"Only one in a thousand adult models has what it takes to be acceptable. Then before being launched to the industry they must be groomed and coached,"* but a good number of the children whose mothers paraded through Walter's agencies were cute enough to model right away. *"No fuss, no muss,"* he commented. *"All they have to do is be themselves, natural and unaffected."* Although Thornton turned down fifty to seventy-five percent of child applicants per week, *"many mothers hated to take "no" for an answer. One of them went on a sit-down strike [in Thornton's office] vainly trying to force a favorable answer."*

Dad organized his child-modeling business in the same manner as he had started his initial business. First, he developed and published a catalog. His lookbooks were sensibly called *Just Kids Models,* the only one in the country. A typical model's page in the catalog would show a photo of the child and often a mocked-up sample print ad to give the client an idea of how great the child would look in their ads. When a child or baby was booked on a modeling job for an ad, just like adult models, Walter received a standard ten percent commission on earnings between seven fifty to as much as ten to fifteen dollars an hour. Children under one year old were paid a standard ten dollars an hour.

Clients seized the opportunity to work with his young models, and more and more frequently, the sample print ads that appeared in *Just Kids Models* catalogs garnered huge numbers of requests to book a child to replicate that exact expression shown in the catalog picture. But those expressions couldn't always be easily duplicated because, well, the expression had been spontaneous. That's when Dad had his next life-changing epiphany.

Why not develop a stock photo service to go along with his booking service? He could further expand his business while at the same time increasing the child model's earning power. He would license his supply of already-made photographs for the client's specific need and use. And since the client was licensing the use of a ready-made photo, this catalog wouldn't be confined to just the New York metropolitan market, it could be distributed internationally! The idea spurred an innovation in the industry.

For the first time, Dad could fulfill the needs of creative assignments without the significant costs involved with booking a photo session. What's more, a child's earning capacity could continue long after her advancing age had shoved her out of the market for the type that made her successful. A photo is timeless. It could provide continued revenue indefinitely, especially so because old catalogs were never recalled, and Walter's clients kept them and commonly ordered from them long after they received newer issues. The New York edition of *Just Kids Models* catalog was so successful that the agency collected pictures of the cutest children from all parts of the country and published a stock-photo-only catalog called *Just Kids Photos*, which he did, in fact, circulate internationally.

The first year Walter sold his catalog for five dollars directly to advertisers who could select one of the photographs and pay the model directly. He made nothing from the money paid to the model. His profit, if any after expenses, would come from the sale of the catalog which he hoped to place with five thousand to six thousand firms annually. Parents of prospective child models paid third parties to have photographs taken and paid the agency $50 ($620 according to the 2023 CPI) for advertising and shipping expenses. That was the only fee and the child would continue to be "registered" with the agency as long as they were available for work. Engagements were not guaranteed, and it was advertised as such. In 1948, several Associated Press interviews that ran throughout the country showed the pros and cons of becoming a catalog model and it was up to the parents to decide if they wanted to invest in them. He handled many kids who had really good earnings, such as the thirteen-year-old model who had been working steadily since she was two, with gross earnings of $10,000 in a year ($130,000 according to the 2023 CPI). "*But, and it's a big but, there is a long list of models who don't make a dime.*" So, if your child wasn't picked to model, "*you wind up in the red to the extent of the cost of your advertising and photographs.*" These were not the words of a con man looking to fleece unsuspecting parents in a *child model racket.*

W alter's restructuring of his empire was taking place against a backdrop of gathering thunderclouds on the show business industry horizon; an ever-intensifying drama that was being played out mostly in Washington, D.C. However, it quickly engulfed all of America—especially Hollywood and the entertainment industry. The U.S. House of Representatives formed the House Un-American Activities Committee (HUAC), soon after WWII ended. HUAC is an acronym that today represents the most poisonous, "tell on your neighbors" era of witch-hunt hysteria that had ever swept the nation.

Our father had always chosen to remain largely apolitical. From a business standpoint, it was the safest, most logical position. But the changing political climate was unavoidable for Walter, when a booklet called *Red Channels: The Report of Communist Influence in Radio and Television* was released in 1950. You couldn't avoid reading about it in newspapers, and hearing and seeing it on radio and television. Walter would witness from the sidelines as many extended friends, associates and show-business colleagues found their names listed amongst the one hundred fifty-one "Red sympathizers" and "commies" that were initially included in the booklet. One hundred seventy additional names were added by 1952, becoming more broadly known as the "Hollywood Blacklist." There were a disproportionate number of African Americans on the list (Josephine Baker, Paul Robeson, Canada Lee, Lena Horne, jazz pianist Hazel Scott, to name a few). And an overwhelming number of the writers and directors who were "named" were Jewish. Racism and anti-Semitism seemed to be at the very root of Red *Channels*. Which is pretty curious when you consider the loudest promoter of the *Red Channels* booklet was Walter Winchell-who was Jewish!

As we mentioned earlier, Jean Muir, who had been the Thornton Agency's first major Hollywood breakout star in the early 1930s, was the very first Hollywood figure to be fired because of her inclusion in the booklet as a suspected commie.

AMERICANS.....
DON'T PATRONIZE REDS!!!!
——•——

YOU CAN DRIVE THE REDS OUT OF
TELEVISION, RADIO AND HOLLY-
WOOD.....

THIS TRACT WILL TELL YOU HOW.

WHY WE MUST DRIVE THEM OUT:

Above: Anti-Communist leaflet distributed in Los Angeles, 1950

In 1950, when General Foods announced that it would be pulling its sponsorship from any television program that featured "controversial persons," the General Foods-sponsored NBC program, *The Aldrich Family*, immediately and very publicly fired Jean Muir. After her firing, Muir voluntarily appeared before HUAC, nearly pleading to be believed, stating under oath:

"I am not a Communist, have never been one, and believe that the Communists represent a vicious and destructive force, and I am opposed to them."

But it was all to no avail. No one was listening—and the long, successful career of Jean Muir was destroyed for good. Author William Manchester called her "a martyr, sacrificed to ignorance and fear as surely as any Salem 'witch' in 1692."

Political greenhorn though he may have been, Walter Thornton was about to experience a deeply damaging takedown of his own, in the form of a personally directed vendetta that would send his life and career into utter chaos. And, in retrospect, he never stood a chance against the toxic trainload that was swiftly headed 'round the bend and aimed directly at him. He never saw it coming.

It is a fact that during this period of time, baby- and child-model rackets were proliferating. As early as 1949, experts were warning parents to watch for scams, particularly from obscure agencies with unknown names that "solicit pictures of children for display in a 'customers' book." Grand promises might cause parents with high expectations to fall victim to these unscrupulous outfits. Sometimes the scams were even bolder with alleged 'photography studio reps' going door to door, claiming to be the exclusive photographer for major modeling agencies interested in recruiting. "Your child has been recommended for acceptance," parents were promised—but first they would have to pay a studio fee for a photo composite. Of course, these con artists had no affiliation with the modeling agencies at all.

We learned that, in 1953, a year before Dad's arrest, several photography studios, who were in no way connected with his agency, lured unsuspecting parents with a pitch that said the child's picture would be kept on file with the Walter Thornton modeling agency in New York City. Several other cases were reported where the salesman told the mother that they were the "exclusive photographer for Walter Thornton" and that her child had been "recommended" by the Thornton modeling agency, but that a large five-picture composite, costing about forty dollars, was required for the agency's use. With this bait, most mothers went on the hook and paid a deposit of about six dollars. It was further represented to them that a modeling contract for her child would be forthcoming in about thirty to sixty days.

The Rockland County district attorney did a series of investigations that were highly publicized. Our dad testified in a deposition that his agency was not affiliated with the photography studios in question; further, he had not seen nor recommended any of the children's photos that those studios said were included in his catalogs and what's more, his catalogs *didn't even use composite photos*. The photos on the *Just Kids* catalogs were standalone shots of the individual child. The Rockland County District Attorney concluded that Walter Thornton Model Publications, Inc., was a reputable business engaged in the publication and distribution of a modeling picture directory which was widely distributed to advertisers and other clients throughout the United States and a number of foreign countries and was not involved in the fraud. Despite the Rockland County DA's words, six months later, Walter was indicted by Queen's County District Attorney T. Vincent Quinn, on many charges, including fraud.

Chapter 23

Trials of a Merchant of Venus

Nancy

"The world...
a stage where every man must play a part.
And mine a sad one."
The Merchant of Venice – by William Shakespeare.
Antonio, Act 1, Scene 1

On January 24, 1954, Walter and ten of his female employees were arrested, handcuffed and hustled from Walter Thornton, Inc.'s Park Avenue offices. The loud explosions from the flashbulbs of tabloid photographers (who had been tipped off) were blinding as the suspects were herded into paddy wagons. Walter was taken to the 108th Precinct police station in Long Island City, NY. Arriving at the facility, he was paraded past another hoard of tabloid press in front of the jail. So, scores of reporters covered the "walks of shame" at both ends of his arrest.

All defendants were briefly detained before being released on bond, awaiting trial on twenty-three counts, which included everything from petty larceny to grand larceny—and, seemingly, everything in between—including conspiracy to defraud and multiple related charges of alleged fraud. "Thornton's technique lay in preying on the hopes and natural pride of parents in their children," DA Quinn explained to the tabloid mob outside the police precinct, as Walter was being booked inside. The media circus that followed, featuring District Attorney Quinn as the ringmaster, was so expertly choreographed with its almost-daily press conferences and banner headlines, that three of the ten arrested agency employees would soon collapse under pressure and agree to testify against their now-former boss, Walter Thornton. There was no precursor to this planned attack on the character and reputation of our father. He had maintained a spotless record as a businessman—and a gentleman—for almost thirty years. Of the hundreds of models he represented, there wasn't even a whisper of scandal, malfeasance or ethics violations. He'd had to sue a few of *them*, when they conveniently "forgot about" the one-to-three-year contracts they'd signed with the Thornton Agency, but he was never sued or had an official complaint filed against him by any of his models.

The prosecution's case against Thornton summarized that he and his staff of agency representatives had falsely *promised* "tender-hearted parents" that if they paid him the thirty-to-fifty-dollar fee to include their children's photographs in his *Just Kids* catalogs, they were *guaranteed* to find employment as models. And that was it. Those were the allegations, despite the critical point that his newspaper advertisements for the *Just Kids* catalogs said, in plain English, "engagements cannot be guaranteed."

In researching this reckless misuse of taxpayers' money for the sake of 'justice', we learned a new word. Language in the charges made by the Queens DA claimed that Walter Thornton had *mulcted* hundreds of gullible parents in Queens, NY. Such an ugly word. Sounds almost painful. The headlines claimed our father was arrested, handcuffed and taken to jail for "mulcting hundreds of *loving parents* out of their hard-earned money." *Merriam-Webster* defines mulct as "**a:** to defraud especially of money; swindle; **b:** to obtain by fraud, duress, or theft."

That was the beginning and end of T. Vincent Quinn's criminal case against Walter Thornton and his staff, as far as the court case went anyway. But that was only one part of the DA office's two-pronged plan. The really effective part was the smear campaign case that was argued in the tabloids over the next five-plus months. It was a vicious masterpiece of personal accusations (not charges) that the DA's office leveled against Walter Thornton daily. And so began the patent frame-up of Walter Thornton, the Monstrous Mulcter of Park Avenue.

The claims that were headlined in the tabloids became truly ludicrous. Statements that our father had never helped *anyone* in the modeling industry. This "so-called Merchant of Venus" was a fraud, a thief, a liar and a racketeer. According to an article in the *New York World-Telegram & Sun* under the title "Stars to Call Thornton a Bust as Booster," with the sub-headline, "Stars Fall on Him:"

"Some of the nation's top glamor queens will be called as witnesses against Walter Thornton, the modeling agent who was not exactly a model citizen.

"Arrested yesterday on an indictment accusing him of running a $600,000 ($6.8 million according to the 2023 CPI) model casting racket. Thornton then was found to be an ex-convict. Police said his fingerprint record disclosed he was sent to Elmira Prison for robbery in 1919, when he was 16. At the time, he was known as John Hammond of Queens.

"Curvaceous Marilyn Monroe, Shelley Winters, Joan Crawford and Lauren Bacall are mentioned by Queens authorities as prospective witnesses. A spokesman for the Queens District Attorney's office said these and other sirens will refute Thornton's claims that he started them on the road to fame and fortune. Thornton [...] allegedly took credit for launching their careers in his sales spiel to clients. District Attorney

T. Vincent Quinn said a six-month investigation showed Thornton had defrauded proud parents of at least $600,000 by 'false representation, that they would obtain lucrative positions in modeling and TV for their children.'

"Thornton, who lives at 5 Tudor Place, is charged with conspiracy to defraud, grand larceny and petty larceny. Assistant District Attorney William Kerwick dug into records at the Supreme Court building in Jamaica [Queens] this afternoon and came up with this information: Late in 1919 Thornton, giving as his address the 57th St. YMCA, pleaded guilty to participating in a $5 stickup of a shoe store at 2 Boulevard, Edgemere, in the Far Rockaway section of Queens. Thornton, who said at the time that he was an orphan from Beaver, Ohio, [along with a] 15-year-old boy, not immediately identified today, were accused of robbing Romeo La Parta [sic] Aug. 3, 1919. Thornton was nabbed in Cleveland. After his return here August 28, 1919, he also was indicted for grand larceny in connection with the theft of money from two rooming house tenants, but this charge was dismissed after he pleaded guilty to the robbery indictment and began an indeterminate term at Elmira.

"Mr. Kerwick said Thornton enlisted in the Army in 1918 [...] but was discharged nine months later after it was discovered he had lied about his age."

The only things in the above article that would survive a fact check were: he did jumpstart Lauren Bacall's career: he was an orphan from Beaver Ohio, he was living at 5 Tudor Place and he did serve and was discharged from the Army (except they had that date wrong). All facts that were well known from Dad's own interviews and advertising. If that wasn't enough, their actions went further, depicting him as a sympathizer of communism. Unflattering photographs of him were prominently showcased on the newspaper's front page. These images were accompanied by headlines intended to implicate other individuals in communist activities, effectively associating his face with communism in the public's perception.

So it's no wonder that after this case was dismissed, our dad would file his own multi-million dollar libel suit against this "newspaper". And it wasn't the only one he'd file.

The DA's game plan was evidently: Attack on all fronts! Hit low, hit hard! Release daily unflattering stories on Thornton to the tabloid press. Keep the story alive. Fan the public outrage. And if you don't have the goods, make 'em up. Be creative! Employ the always-popular *evil twin plot twist* by inventing sixteen-year-old John Hammond! DA Quinn, and his Assistant DA John Kerwick, continued to add additional flourishes that were so fantastic they seemed to be trying to top themselves. Some of these revelations were: "He claims to be a famous modeling agent" and "He was kicked out of the army for lying." (He, of course, was honorably discharged.) Our file of newspaper/magazine coverage of the spurious "Child Model Racket" has grown quite voluminous.

Our father's arrest made international news, including the remote Australian town newspaper, The *Barrier-Miner* of Broken Hill, New South Wales, where it appeared at the top of the front page on January 27, 1954.

THE MERCHANT OF VENUS HEAD ON FRAUD CHARGES

New York, Tues.: Walter Thornton, a nationally-known agent for models, was arrested yesterday and charged that he defrauded ambitious parents of 600,000 dollars (£268,000).

He is alleged to have made unfulfilled promises of television and modelling fame to their children. Thornton claimed that he aided scores of Hollywood actresses to stardom

Thornton, who was once a bricklayer, established his model agency in 1934 and styled himself "The Merchant of Venus."

tribu ed among big advertisers.

He induced parents to have their children's photographs published in the catalogue at 50 dollars (£22) each.

Lightning

To our dad's credit, he did not take this outlandish arrest lying down. He called out Quinn's frame-up in multiple interviews, including the *Time* magazine article in May of 1954, just before his trial began, where our dad called Quinn a *"publicity-hungry politician."* He said, *"District Attorney Quinn hasn't got a case in the world. It's merely for publicity. He's under indictment himself, and he's trying to make everyone forget about it."* But he was like a person trying to be heard while screaming underwater. And that last sentence from our dad really sums up the rationale behind the whole Quinn charade.

Quinn had been the Assistant to U.S. Attorney General Tom C. Clark under Harry S. Truman, from 1945 to 1949. During that tenure, they had supervised the prosecution of the "Hollywood 10" in 1947, as well as the case against Iva Toguri as the fictitious "Tokyo Rose' (which she never was) in 1949. Then, in quick succession, came his period of being a Member of Congress, aborted by his early resignation and retreat back to Queens, where he was installed as District Attorney.

We learned that in 1953, almost exactly a year to the day before our father's arrest, T. Vincent Quinn was in the headlines—only this time, he was the subject of them. Quinn had an open federal indictment hanging over his own head; meaning he could be placed under arrest at any time. It seems that after he resigned his seat as U.S. Congressman (one could easily assume it *was the reason* for his early resignation) he was accused on twenty-eight counts of "accepting improper tax fees while in office" (in layman's terms, graft or bribery or money under the table). Evidently his legal practice in Washington remained open while Quinn was in Congress. He was giving legal advice to clients about their upcoming business with the federal government, *while he was an elected official in that federal government*, serving as a member of Congress. He was in large trouble.

He was just two years into his term as DA, and two years away from re-election, so he would have to campaign with the indictment hanging over his head.

So he set out to make over his image, to position himself as a tough-on-crime, stand-up guy. He really needed something sparkly with which to distract the voters, and a top player in the glamorous world of modeling is pretty sparkly. Throw in swindled mothers and babies and well, you can't get much sparklier than that! As Walter Winchell once said, "The way to become famous fast is to throw a brick at someone who *is* famous." Since the sensationalistic New York tabloids were the only source of news for millions of New Yorkers, it was nearly impossible to remove the stench after a targeted, tabloid feeding frenzy like the one Quinn had orchestrated against our dad. Ruined lives became more grist for the media mill. If it was a big-name celebrity or political figure, the tabloids could stretch it out into a one- or two-month blizzard of headlines and stories. Our father's frame-up was an exceptional one since, start to finish, it remained in the headlines for just under six months. And then, just as quickly as the story had come, it totally disappeared. After which, aside from the ruined life and career of the man, it was as if nothing had ever happened at all.

Chapter 24

Autos-da--fé

Adriana

"What a day, what a day,
for an auto-da-fĕ,
It's a lovely day for drinking and
for watching people fry!"

Lyrics from the McCarthy-era, allegorical Broadway musical, *Candide* (1956), by Leonard Bernstein, John Latouche, Lillian Hellman and Dorothy Parker—all of whom found themselves on the "Hollywood Blacklist." [*Auto-da-fĕ:* the burning of a heretic during the fifteenth-century Spanish Inquisition.]

The Child Model Racket Trial" began on May 7, 1954 at the Queens County Court building in Long Island City, Queens, New York. The prosecution "witnesses" against Walter Thornton consisted of a steady parade of aggrieved Queens mothers. It was reported in local coverage of the trial that Judge Peter G. Farrell needed to bang his gavel to restore order in the court, more than once, when court spectators erupted in laughter at some of the very coached, overly dramatic, and yet, inconsistent testimony of some of the mothers who were milking their own moments in the spotlight. Each of them, in a curiously similar fashion, testified that they had paid their thirty-five dollars—and their child hadn't received a single inquiry. Unfortunately for the prosecution, much as Kerwick tried to elicit from them that Thornton and his agents had <u>promised</u> them employment from their children's photo placement in the catalogs, not a single one of their witnesses testified to that having been the case.

"The agent I spoke to said that they had discovered Peggy Ann Garner and made her a star," said Evelyn Hertz, 47, of Sunnyside, Queens. "No, they never promised any jobs to us," Mrs. Hertz testified. "But I thought we would at least get some calls, and we never got any."

The twelve members of the jury, according to the *Daily News*, appeared "bored and incredulous." Some of Kerwick's questioning of the heartbroken parents made it sound as if he was spoon-feeding them exactly what he wanted them to say, only to have them veer off-script, offering information that was far more helpful to the defense. When that happened, ADA Kerwick would quickly conclude their testimonies and summon the next witness. Reportedly, cracks were beginning to appear in Kerwick's previously stony composure as he surely recognized their "Child Model Racket" case was falling to pieces. The sheer volume of poorly coached witnesses had taken the proceedings into the realm of a stage farce. And there were the other witnesses, the parents of those children who did get modeling jobs through the *Just Kids* catalog, who testified in Dad's defense. In all, thirty-six aggrieved parents took the stand for the prosecution of Walter Thornton—before the "trial" came to an awkward halt.

In trying to unravel our dad's takedown, one of the most troublesome claims we'd uncovered was the purported fingerprint evidence implicating our father in a thirty-five-year-old adolescent crime wave, under the assumed name of "John Hammond." Quinn told the press that his Assistant DA Kerwick had somehow linked Walter Thornton's booking fingerprints to those of a stick-up robber in 1919, while "poking around the Queens County Court building in Jamaica" on the very day they arrested Walter Thornton! That Quinn/Kerwick were able to effortlessly blend this "evil twin" side story into the mix is remarkable. Since there was no organized, searchable database for fingerprints in 1954—let alone in 1918—this makes it not only remarkable, it makes it unbelievable.

Dead End to Penthouse: Thornton Rose Hard Way

By JOHN E. SUTPHIN

Walter Thornton, the model agency mogul with a penthouse and a six-figure income, was a homeless Dead End kid 35 years ago, desperate enough to go hunting for money with a borrowed gun.

Thornton—or John Hammond, as he was known in those days—went to jail in 1919 after pleading guilty to armed robbery. It appears to have been his only brush with the law until he was indicted for gypping parents in a child model racket.

Dusty papers dug out of the Queens district attorney's files tell an interesting story of the Thornton that Broadway never knew . . . no, nor Hollywood, either.

* * *

JUDGING by the affidavit that Thornton signed back in 1919, he was born John Hammond in Chillicothe, Ohio. His boyhood was spent in Beaver, Ohio, a suburb

WALTER THORNTON

a bustling summer colony. Hammond had a gun—he said later he borrowed it, but was never pressed to identify the lender.

* * *

THE TWO SNEAKED into a rooming house and rifled the belongings of two summer boarders—Samuel J. Pinskey of the Bronx and Max Fabian of Manhattan. From there they went to Romeo La Peruta's shoe store at No. 2 Boulevard and stuck up Romeo. They got $5.

After the Queens holdup, the boys fled to Cleveland, where young Hammond knew his way around.

They tried another stickup there, but the victim was stubborn. He wouldn't hand over any money, even after Hammond fired two revolver shots into the floor to scare him.

The shots brought the cops.

* * *

QUEENS WANTED Hammond badly enough to extradite him. He

Above: Meet John Hammond (New York Daily News, January 26, 1954)

Quinn said that Walter Thornton was a fraudulent businessman, a serial grifter who'd operated outside the law all his life. His deluxe, high-flying lifestyle was all a mask for his *real* persona, that of a lying, felonious, mulcting ex-convict named John Hammond. The DA's office had prepared a file folder of these and other bombshells it had concocted that could be dispersed in a drip-drip-drip fashion to the tabloid press, lasting for the months before, during and after the trial. This would surely shift the attention off of any potential federal indictments on Quinn.

The "John Hammond" accusations were never substantiated in any way. They were never uttered at his trial (not that they would have been admissible). But, for the record, we contacted the Elmira Reformatory in Upstate New York. It remains today as Elmira Correctional Facility. As per our recent records request, no records were found for Walter Clarence Thornton at Elmira. They did find a few John Hammonds in their files, but the dates did not align properly with our father's would-be evil twin.

From the day the headline blizzard began, the Queens DA's office proclaimed, with certainty, that they had solid evidence of Walter Thornton's shady past, as well as his unsavory present. As for the Hollywood leading ladies that had been listed by Kerwick "as prospective witnesses," he could have inserted the name Minnie Mouse in the list if he'd wanted to. It wouldn't have mattered since none of the names he did give were ever called in to testify.

I'm trying not to sound too "hard-boiled" in recounting Quinn's plot to decimate our father's reputation. But Quinn was out to get him, using any means he could invent. Walter had the full weight against him of a corrupt, vicious district attorney who, cornered by his own impending indictments and needing to divert attention while looking tough on crime, was intent on ruining our father. If convicted on all the prosecution's felony charges, our father would have been facing a decades-long sentence in prison. When we interviewed Arlene Dahl in 2021, one of our ten questions had been whether she had any memories about being subpoenaed to fly to New York to testify against her former agent, she responded:

WHAT? [emphasis hers] *I would NEVER have done something like that! Why would I say the man who made me a famous model didn't make me a famous model? It's absurd and I would have never even considered such a thing. No, I have no memory of any such thing.*

After four weeks of the trial rambling on, it seems obvious Judge Farrell was not impressed by the performance. According to one contemporaneous accounting, "Kerwick basically threw his hands in the air when directly confronted by Judge Farrell to provide any 'actual evidence' against the defendants." Back in the first week after the arrests, Quinn mentioned the phrase "FBI surveillance tapes" or "wiretapping" as being their best proof. And so the prosecution attempted to enter its "hours of FBI recordings" into evidence. Understandably, Judge Farrell said he'd be most interested in hearing this evidence. On June 2, 1954, court proceedings went into recess for the day, in order for Judge Farrell to listen to some of these *explosive* wiretap recordings in his chambers, in order to decide on their admissibility.

When the court reconvened the following morning, Judge Farrell thanked the jury members for their dedication and for fulfilling their civic duty. Then he got down to business. He completely dismissed all charges against the defendants and shamed the prosecution for pressing such a dubious case against Walter Thornton and his employees. As the judge stated in his dismissal of the Child Model Racket trial, "There is absolutely no proof that any law has been broken here, and even if there had been, this would not be the jurisdiction for such charges."

The *Daily News* summed up the trial thusly: "After seventeen days of dreary, meandering testimony, a disgusted Queens County judge threw the Walter Thornton child-model case out of court." Judge Farrell used the word "reprehensible" in his angry dismissal of this expensive, baseless waste of taxpayer-funded resources. Now, the judge was no fan of the idea of the child-model casting directory, given how easily unscrupulous businesses with no name or wide distribution could fool parents, but there was no law against it so he made clear that it was the legislature's job to create an appropriate law to regulate it.

Ted Koti

Walter Thornton (right), the model agent, with his lawyer, Congressman Eugene J. Keogh, outside court in Long Island City, Queens, yesterday.

Thornton in Court, Wins Plea Delay

March 5 was set yesterday in Queens County Court for Walter Thornton to plead to an indictment unsealed Monday charging him with conspiracy to defraud, grand larceny and petty larceny in connection with pictures of would-be child models. Mr. Thornton, who publishes a directory of models at 270 Park Ave., was scheduled to plead yesterday, but his request for a delay was granted. He is free on $2,500 bail.

Happy photos of Walter being surrounded by his team of exonerated employees, one kissing him on his cheek, appeared in the very back pages of a few of the tabloids. T. Vincent Quinn did not organize a press conference for this occasion. But, spoiler alert, he did continue his campaign for re-election. Alas, much to his dismay, his Congressional indictments as well as his antics in the Thornton case and others, led the Queens County Democratic Executive Committee to find him unsuitable as their nominee (which went to State Senator Frank O'Connor) and so he wasn't even able to run in the election.

I t was Adriana who first mentioned a possible connection between our father's takedown and the "bankrupt investor" image. *"Think about it. If you piece together all the other terrible things they made up about him, I think Quinn doctored that image,"* she said. *"They found a couple of unrelated, old modeling photos of Dad and doctored them to bolster their case that our father was a fake—an irresponsible businessman all his life. Maybe they planned to share them with the press as a weapon for them to use against him? Could Quinn have intended to send the doctored images to the New York tabloid editors, but then got preempted when the case was dismissed?"*

Given how vicious and specious Quinn had been with the case against Walter, we didn't think it was unlikely at all. But, like so much about this whole affair, we'll never entirely know for sure.

Chapter 25

Framed

Nancy

O ur conclusion was simply this: Walter Thornton was framed. But the fictitious headlines had served their purpose. They planted the fertile seed of suspicion in the public consciousness that Walter Thornton had been illicitly tied to a case involving grand larceny and babies. He was an outcast. Based upon...absolutely nothing, other than a corrupt district attorney trying to save his skin. Going through his final, sealed box of legal and business papers, we were privy to Walter's downward spiral, following this sad episode. We were able to discover our father's own thoughts relating to the fall of the Merchant of Venus. And he was pissed. Along with winding down most of Walter Thornton, Inc, he spent the next four years, post-frame-up, mostly focused on his several lawsuits against Hearst & Co. He'd plainly been libeled—and someone should pay for it.

Suing the Hearst Corporation was not something one took on casually in the mid-twentieth century. It's impossible to overstate the influence, wealth and power that a litigant against Hearst would have been up against. Even with its decades-long pattern of libelous smears, the Hearst Corporation was infrequently sued for libel and/or defamation of character. It's more than likely that in cases where Hearst was clearly at fault, many suits disappeared after they were quietly settled out of court.

Dad wanted to get his good name and reputation back, at all costs. In addition to filing suit against the Hearst Corporation, he filed separate libel suits against *Newsday*, the *New York World-Telegram & Sun* and the *New York Herald Tribune*, Hearst's flagship New York broadsheet.

He filed two additional suits against individual reporters who wrote some of the most slanderous pieces about him. One was Paul Meskiel (aka "Paul S. Meskil"), a sometime fiction writer, whose 1953 paperback, *Sin Pit*, had hit the drugstore pulp fiction racks a few months before he began writing tabloid "hit pieces" about Walter Thornton. The other was Samuel P. Crowther III, a long-time company man with the Hearst Corporation. We assume that our dad had pinpointed Crowther as the point man of the entire Hearst offensive against him.

Walter's various lawsuits were eventually either dropped or inexplicably dismissed for "filing errors" and nebulous statutes-of-limitation. Before he threw any more money at it, his keen instinct for self-preservation and self-reinvention told him that his reign as "The Merchant of Venus" had been played out. Besides, he was still dealing with his health issues so he knew it was time to go.

We found very few people who knew our father in that period who were still living. More than once, our inquiries would be mailed back, stamped "DECEASED," or we would find their current whereabouts via Findagrave.com.

Our search did fortuitously lead us to the first cousin of our half-sister: Kirby Kooluris. I felt an instant warmth of kinship when I called him, out of the blue, around 2015. We had never met or spoken before. He was living in Palm Beach, Florida. Though he was only a young—and highly precocious—child in the 1950s, little Kirby was very much on the scene in the waning days of his Uncle Walter's thirty-four-year run in New York City. In the days leading up to Dad's departure for Mexico—essentially, forever—Kirby recalled the image of his Uncle Walter sitting before his roaring, alabaster-mantled, tri-story fireplace as he threw papers by the fistful—letters, photographs, newspaper articles—into the flames. Kirby recalled, "*I remember the fireplace burning furiously...because I can't recall them ever using that fireplace at any other time.*" Walter's ex-wife Judy had divorced him and moved into the matching penthouse next door a few years earlier.

The Tudor City complex was built in 1926 as the very first residential skyscraper community in the world. The triple-height "grand parlors" of the Windsor Tower's three matching penthouses have floor-to-ceiling windows, with the Thornton unit facing southeasterly, toward the East River, with views of the midtown Manhattan skyline as well. But inside Kirby remembered a vacant grandiosity about the place as most of Walter's personal effects had already been carted off to a storage facility in the Bronx. He seems to have wanted to just put it all behind him, starting afresh, somewhere new. Box it up. Throw it out. Burn it.

After over thirty years in New York City, the sands of Walter Thornton's hourglass had trickled through and he was done. Four years of lawsuits and trials had severely depleted his resources. He still had a large, controlling interest in the chain of charm schools in Canada that bore his name. But in the U.S., his name and reputation had actually become a liability to him. The months leading up to his Uncle Walter's farewell stood in stark contrast to Kirby's fond memories of his uncle from earlier, happier times.

Kirby recalls him often being surrounded by children, for whom he'd act out crazy routines to entertain. "*He was a very sunny fellow, and he didn't talk down to kids,*" he recalled. "*I have a mental image of him at some family event, where there were many children. Uncle Walter was surrounded by a half-moon of laughing children, while he performed an improvisational skit, wherein he held a zither behind his back and would pluck a chord, followed by him dramatically 'pulling faces' that the chords represented ...sad...confused...ecstatic,*" Kirby recalled. "*We kids thought he was hilarious.*"

As something of a sardonic twist, Walter chose to leave New York City, forever, on April 1, 1958—April Fool's Day. He would not have to suffer through a joyless, sparsely attended birthday party for him on April 3, his fifty-fifth—the kind of "celebration" that had happened since the trial. For years before that, at least since the early 1930s, Walter Thornton's birthday celebrations had been lavish, annual public spectacles. One year it was held at the Stork Club, Manhattan's most glittering celebrity gathering place. The parties had been invariably covered in the press.

Though he'd only briefly visited there one time before, our father decided to move to Guadalajara, Mexico. Walter's choice of venue for his next chapter seemed, on the surface, a "stick-a-pin-on-a-map" type of relocation choice, though he'd clearly researched the essentials. He knew that he was done with the United States. He'd witnessed the carnage of the McCarthy Era first-hand and just wanted out. Mexico would serve as something of a safe haven, politically, after the poisonously fraught climate throughout much of America in the 1950s. Guadalajara had an international airport and was a fairly short flight away from Los Angeles, if necessary. The tropical climate seemed too good to be true; and the cost of living there was dramatically lower than anywhere in the U.S.

According to our mother, he thought it would be a good place to restart his business, too, on a much smaller scale. He envisioned starting a charm school in Guadalajara. The concept of "charm schools" in the U.S. is now considered fairly archaic, sort of quaintly antique. It is a rather sweet notion that one could attend a school that dispensed charm. But they were quite popular in the U.S. until around the 1970s. John Robert Powers was the first to develop them on a wide-scale basis; a company that bears his name is still in business (he sold his brand in the 1960s to a conglomerate). It seems there is still a market for charm in this world, which is nice to know. There are worse things to dispense than charm. Our dad seemed to think so. In any case, instead of charm schools, he found love and that's where we come from.

Chapter 26

Suspicion

Adriana

By the early 2020s, the "bankrupt investor" Walter Thornton images had become the oft-used representation of desperation caused by the stock market crash of 1929. Countless historians, filmmakers and documentarians have relied upon them. History-oriented chat rooms, social media groups and websites continue to employ the images as the clearest personification of the crash. "The man in the bankrupt investor picture symbolizes every irresponsible fool who caused the stock market to crash in the first place," a Reddit commenter confidently opined recently. Not only has "bankrupt Investor" Walter Thornton come to represent the 1929 crash, the two images also seem to act as an archetype of both the generation of freewheeling wild speculation that came before it—as well as the generation that came after it, often representing the Great Depression itself. They're highly versatile, as iconic images go.

Since we've been following the popularity of the two images on Google for nearly twenty years, our family keeps close tabs on the rise—and rise—of the number of online usages. The last time we performed a Google image search for the bracketed term "The Great Depression," both "bankrupt investor" images appeared very early in the results (not to mention, when searching "stock market crash 1929" and "crash 1929"). Not only that, they've made it recently into the pages of both the *Wall Street Journal* and the *New York Times*. We have to admit that we Thorntons, even after all we'd learned, still loved the car photos and tried to find a way to continue to hang onto them, if only for their sentimental value. We would sometimes place his most recent portrait as well as the framed car image on his regular seat, the chair at the head of a long dinner table, especially at Christmas dinners.

We have each had it hanging proudly in our homes, thanks to Nancy. Soon after we discovered the image, she'd sent us each an oversized, framed copy of the group shot. We were proud of it and considered it a blessing. We had no desire to renounce it. We weren't looking to dismantle a beloved family icon. But as we slowly learned about Dad's takedown and the possibility that the images may have played a part, it made us almost involuntarily shrink away from it.

"*Y*ou *know what? I'm finally convinced that the sign is a total fake. Take a fresh look at "bankrupt investor" and imagine it without the sign. And study both photos side by side,*" Nancy told me in an early-morning phone call in 2020. "*I've studied those images a thousand times by now,*" she said. "*I didn't want to admit it aloud, but I've always found there was something off about it. And I finally know what it is: it's that sign. It is Photoshopped or something.*"

"*Photoshop wasn't even invented until decades later,*" I said. "*Back then they called it 'retouching'. They would literally etch, or airbrush, alterations onto the film negative.*" But once she *did* say it out loud, there was no denying it anymore. The sign is oddly angled on the car, and in two different placements in the shots. How is it even staying balanced on the roadster? The perspective of the lettering seems somehow skewed. The sign itself almost glows; the lighting doesn't quite match the circumstances of an October street in midtown Manhattan. In the rain.

N ancy sent me an email in 2020 saying, "*Why don't we get these two photos professionally examined, to see if we can prove they've been doctored?*" She was right. Rather than continue in our helpless frustration, we decided it was time to take some constructive action.

When I was in law school, I was aware of the use of forensic photographic analysis. Such highly skilled experts are frequently cited in legal cases. I wanted to find the top expert in all of America. I contacted a few of my former colleagues for recommendations on finding one of the most respected forensic analysts in the photographic field. A name that was frequently mentioned was retired First Lieutenant Eric Johnson of Forensic Photo Analysis Services in East Lansing, Michigan.

His testimony has been relied upon—internationally—in hundreds of legal cases throughout his thirty-year career with the Michigan State Police. His expertise lay in literally putting images under the microscope and analyzing every pixel of a given photograph or negative—and then arriving at professional conclusions. We sent him the two digitally largest-sized copies of the photographs we had. We hired him to authenticate whether the two images were actual—or not. Were they ever manipulated? Retouched? Was the sign an "add?"

Our research shows that there are no existing original negatives for either image. There is also no credited photographer, nor an original source, given location or confirmed date. It seems to be rather nebulously dated "October 30, 1929." Or it might be captioned either "Black Tuesday" (10/29/29) or "Black Thursday" (10/24/29) when it is reprinted/posted elsewhere. So, take your pick.

As we awaited the forensics results, we continued to go to the next level in our research. We both agreed that in a history-correction mission, the "top authority" would be the U.S. Library of Congress in Washington D.C., to see what (if any) information they could provide, related to the two images. At that point we'd grown accustomed to research dead-ends and/or apathy on the part of apparently understaffed research facilities. To us, we had always assumed that the Library of Congress was some sort of faceless, untouchable monolith. It is not. Anyone can access its collection and enlist the help of some of

America's top research librarians. And sometimes, the fates align and you cross paths with someone dedicated and equipped to point the way to the answers you're seeking.

Our emailed information query was directed to research librarian Jonathan Eaker at the U.S. Library of Congress, Prints & Photographs Division. Thankfully, Jonathan took a special interest in the car images and provided invaluable aid in trying to figure out the real story behind the photos. *"There seems to be a slight halo around the sign. That makes me think someone edited it. Can't say for sure of course, but I'm strongly wondering if this was meant as an ad for Chrysler,"* he wrote to us. He even presented the images to his colleagues at the Library of Congress and the pictures became, according to Jonathan, the subject for lively lunchtime discussion. *"We have a monthly "learning hour" for staff in our division and they wanted to hear some research stories and this is probably the most interesting I've had in the last year,"* he wrote, after he and some of his fellow researchers in the Prints and Photographs Division noted the questionable nature of the signs straightaway. *"I doubt most people would look so nonchalant about their financial ruin,"* he added.

Based upon his extensive, electronic search, Jonathan concluded that the bankrupt investor images made their first-ever appearance in the public in 1973, in an obscure British textbook, published by the Open University. The book is entitled *Between Two Wars* and the image was in "Arts: A Third Level Course, War and Society." Jonathan was able to confidently conclude that there is no known usage of either of the images in print *anywhere prior to 1973*. How the image ended up in England in 1973 is anyone's guess. But "bankrupt investor" never appeared in print before then—and then not again until 1990.

And that's good enough for us.

Chapter 27

The Turning Tide

Nancy

O ur feelings toward "bankrupt investor" had pivoted to resentment. I couldn't help but view it with suspicion and doubt. Had it been a tool forged to destroy our father's reputation? It seemed to fit Quinn's pattern of falsifying evidence and witnesses. If paying and/or strong-arming his various "witnesses" was standard protocol for him, then doctoring photos for nefarious reasons would hardly be a stretch. All New York tabloids of that era would employ photographic retouchers, whose job involved nothing *but* doctoring the photos that appeared in their respective newspapers; often so crudely that they came off as comical. The photographic editing department at any one of those *scandal sheets* could etch a sign into a negative photographic image in no time flat.

We've watched its progression escalate into an iconic status, almost like the stock market itself, with its regular appearances on Reddit, Facebook, X (formerly Twitter) and beyond. Our father's face certainly appears in—and on—a lot of books, too. We've counted fourteen printed books (so far) with the image included, usually on the cover. In 2013, my nephew, Ivan, hurried home from the first day of his junior year in high school and showed one of his new textbooks to Adriana, asking, "*Isn't that Grandpa?*" And, yes, it was him—in Ivan's eleventh-grade U.S. history textbook, *American Anthem: Modern American History* (2007 edition). The caption for it reads:

"**Fallen on Hard Times**: A Wall Street speculator (above) tries to sell his car after losing his wealth in the stock market crash. Margin calls left such investors desperate for cash. What other effects did the stock market crash have on individuals?"

"Bankrupt investor" had fully graduated into the history books. It was being used to teach high schoolers their American History. Officially sanctioned, for posterity. Another book with the image on its cover has quite the pedigree, too: (Atheneum Books for Young Readers, 2002).

Especially confounding for us was the sudden appearance of "bankrupt investor" Walter Thornton on the cover of the 2021 edition of *The Great Crash 1929*. Originally published in 1955, this book has never been out of print. To this day, John Kenneth Galbraith's book is considered to be the definitive overview of the crash and its aftermath. It seems almost like the official anointing of the "bankrupt investor" photograph (the group shot) as <u>the</u> de facto image of the Wall Street Crash of 1929. Doesn't it actually matter that the presumed story behind this image is completely apocryphal?

John Kenneth Galbraith
The Great Crash 1929

Above: The current (2021) edition of J.K. Galbraith's 1955 classic, The Great Crash 1929.

Ironically, our father died the very year the "bankrupt investor" image made its American television and print debut, in 1990, when it first appeared in the PBS *American Experience* documentary film, *The Crash of 1929*. "Bankrupt investor" appears in the documentary, used in a photographic montage of images from the stock market crash era.

The narration as the solo image is introduced is handed over to John Kenneth Galbraith, himself. He was, much owing to his best-selling book on the crash, considered to be the go-to expert on the subject. The "bankrupt investor" image is prominently introduced in a lengthy, slow zoom-in shot in the documentary, as Galbraith intones:

"There's nothing unique about this. It's something that happens every twenty or thirty years, because that is about the length of the financial memory...that it requires for a new set of 'suckers,' if you will; a new set of people capable of the wonderful self-delusion to come in and imagine that they have a new and wonderful fix on the future." (CLOSE-UP of Walter Thornton.)

Thus, it became engraved upon the public consciousness that Walter Thornton emblemized the "suckers, if you will" of the pre-Depression years. There would, however, be comments on Reddit that would boost our confidence in what we were suspecting:

"Photo looks fake to me. The sign has almost certainly been placed in afterwards; there is also some strange pixilation in the background just above the car horn. Interesting how a photo like this was created. It does seem to me that the sign was crafted after the photo was taken. It just doesn't look real: it's too well positioned for the camera. The wording has no perspective (it looks face-on, yet the card implies that it is at an angle) and it's just hanging in space, without any form of support."

Another said: "Only thing is that it doesn't look real. What was that sign made of? Cardboard? How was the sign attached to the car? Why doesn't it cast a shadow? Why is the lighting on the sign so flat? I think that's an early example of photoshopping."

"Damn, they had floating photoshopped signs back then?"

As soon as we learned the grisly details of his 1954 takedown, we knew what our goal had to be: to reveal the truth behind our father's amazing first life, restore his tarnished name and reputation, and prove he was never a "bankrupt investor" nor a mulcter. Learning of his out-of-the-blue takedown, twenty-five years after the stock market crash had definitely complicated matters. But we weren't about to give up now. My point being that, even if it were someone else's father in "bankrupt investor", we'd be just as concerned to learn that *any* well-known American image was misleading and, yet, had never been called into question. Imagine finding out the famous flag-raising at Iwo Jima photo was actually shot in a studio and all the soldiers were male models.

As we scrolled through literally thousands of online comments about Walter Thornton and/or the "bankrupt investor", it saddened us to see that people were "talking trash" about our dad. There is so much supposition involved when viewing the two images. By far, the greatest number of assumptions about the "bankrupt investor" scenario are that these two photographs literally and factually reflect the actual circumstances of the spendthrift gambler named Walter Thornton. After all, that had been our first take on them.

Adriana and I were becoming more and more determined that something had to be done. And evidently, it would have to be done by us. Maybe it *was* possible to correct the history books? That wouldn't be easy with all the various comments and assumptions that appeared online. Two particular reactions were going to be really tough to try and refute. The first was the people who were thrilled at the "bankrupt investor's" comeuppance. The second was the group that honestly believed that the solo shot depicted the man talking on a 1929 cell phone. How do you even *begin* to reason with that?

We knew we were about to poke a rather cantankerous bear by taking on the internet with our amended view of "bankrupt investor". Our hopes were low that we could even make a dent in the world's fixed perception of our father's most famous image. But the idea had been hatched and we were ready to give it a go—one site at a time. We felt we needed to at least try.

Our father deserved no less than that. We compiled and divided a list of every known, prominent internet usage of "bankrupt investor" and decided to try to respond to a few of them per week. We'd written a brief, two-paragraph-long, customizable reply to the sites that used or discussed the "bankrupt investor" images, introducing ourselves as the daughters of the man in the photos:

"I am one of the six surviving children of Walter Thornton (1903-1990), the man in the two "bankrupt investor" images. Walter Thornton was one of the most highly in-demand male models on the roster of the John Robert Powers Agency from 1926-31. There is no factual confirmation as to the date, nor a recorded photographer, source or location—nor are there any known, extant negatives for the "bankrupt investor" photos.

Our father attained worldwide fame in the early 1930s as "The Merchant of Venus," incorporating the very first photographic advertisement modeling agency in America, the Walter Thornton Model Agency, less than a year after the stock market crash.

He is historically credited as the man who "invented" the pinups of WWII.

It is also possible that these images may have been doctored, with the sign added at a later date. His widow, our mother Candelaria, survives him as well."

We started with one particular Reddit group online (with over eight million followers) that had posted the solo image, a copy of which had been garishly colorized. Someone had made the car a #2 pencil yellow color. The picture had received over thirty-two thousand six hundred upvotes and had been shared over nine hundred times.

There were also over six hundred comments. We commented on that photo posting. The initial response was underwhelming. It was as if people didn't want to believe—for starters—that a man born in 1903 could possibly have six still-living children—and a widow—as of 2023. This comment sort of illustrates the gist of feedback we were getting, "He was born in 1903. You couldn't be his children unless your [sic] like 150!"

"Like most people who get ahead in America, it seems like he was just a lying POS. Studies have found that . Capitalism is built to allow these types of people to 'succeed,'" commented another. "Bankrupt investor" has gone through something of a modern twist of late, being used to represent the bursting of the crypto-currency bubble. "Just wait till the crypto Ponzi scheme hits the ceiling and all the peasants are left in ruins," said a recent one. Different signs are frequently added. Different heads are added to the bankrupt investor's body.

We did receive a few nice comments, too, such as a sympathetic respondent who said, "I can understand why you must be frustrated, since it is your dad. GOOD LUCK telling your story!" Some of them suggested we write a book about Walter Thornton. Others suggested we should *read* a book about Walter Thornton, since we clearly didn't know what the hell we were talking about.

We discovered the aggressive downside of the online "community" and its anonymous, often contentious, nature. We approached, hat-in-hand, our main intention being to simply correct the record. We presumed our newfound information would be welcomed in adding context to these now-infamous images. But in some instances, we were suddenly cast in the roles of a couple of lying troublemakers. Or out-and-out fakes. It's not uncommon to have our posted comments on the image questioned, doubted or even utterly dismissed. Yes, we've had our words labeled "#FAKENEWS."

One thing is clear: Web commenters, generally speaking, are very reluctant to forsake these two images as fakeries. I think it's heavily weighted in human nature, in that most humans do not like to be fooled—especially historian humans.

My dad was very much on my mind, while daydreaming in the check-out line of my supermarket when Adriana texted me with a message marked "urgent": *"CHECK YOUR EMAIL. RESULTS FROM PHOTO FORENSICS LAB!"* I rushed home and sat down at my computer, feeling as if my heart was going to jump out of my chest.

Chapter 28

Ergo

Adriana

N ancy called me when she returned from the supermarket. "*I haven't looked at it yet*," I told her. "*I wanted us to read it togeth-er.*" "*Good,*" she replied. "*I'm prepared for anything. I swear, nothing surprises me anymore.*" We both got situated at our computers to read the results of the photographic forensic analysis at the same time. "*Okay, go,*" I said. We each opened the email from Lieutenant Johnson. The professional conclusions regarding the two images were contained within a two-page document. The presentation was fairly clinical and clearly well-informed. The analytical mention of the sign in the images leapt out at first glance; finally, some expert evidence to prove that maybe you can't believe everything you read:

"The only thing I find troublesome is that the sign in Image B [The Solo Image] is bowed in the center; the top bows away from the camera position, and the bottom bows toward the camera position. Any bowing in the center of a sign would typically be the same on the top and bottom – no different than bending a thin piece of cardboard. Based on the position and angle of the sign, it seems unlikely the sign would be bowed in that manner without showing some distortion in the center."

The forensic results were, for the record, "inconclusive." While I was at first disappointed to read that word, I was told that it only meant the lab was unable to either conclusively prove or disprove that the images had been doctored. However, it bolstered our theory to see that the sign in the photos had "irregularities." This was the first solid evidence we had that the sign was sincerely odd-looking. It seems a fair assumption that the photos of the man and the car have been doctored with an added sign.

One thing that still remains especially vexing for us: Why is our father's name nearly always part of the title/caption? We suppose if the image appeared (with the added sign) the day after it was taken, say, in one of the tabloids, a reporter could have asked him his name, thereby providing the man with an identity. But we knew that was not the case because neither of the images appeared in the press in 1929, nor at any point, anywhere else until 1973. His name would have had to have been specifically, deliberately tied to the two images at some point. But when? And for what reason? Who would have benefitted from this image of Walter Thornton, the failed financier? There would have been a less-than-zero percent chance that Chrysler would employ such a crude message to lure potential customers. Besides, in late October of 1929 any Chrysler ad would have been pushing its 1930 models—*not* the 1929 models. The photos without the signs might well have been taken in 1928 as illustrator templates for an ad about the '29 Imperial, whether they were ultimately used or not (though not with 1929 license plates). The same thing could be logically said if they were illustrator templates for a hat or a suit manufacturer.

A hat ad is a likely possibility. In the late 1920s, Walter Thornton was acknowledged as "The Dobbs Hat Man." His cranium was so demanded by hat companies of that era, he is found in multiple hat advertisements, as early as 1926 and as late as 1931. His Dobbs ad in *Vanity Fair* came out two years before the crash. His two, full-page Knapp Felt ads for the *Saturday Evening Post* appeared in the immediate months after the crash. Which is what leads us to believe that the two "bankrupt investor" images (without the sign) were intended to be part of a hat ad campaign. They look like they were illustrator's template photos that could be turned into lithographic advertisements or illustrations.

Note how all the men in the foreground are also perfectly hatted, with fedoras. Most of the younger, Central Casting street-kids at the perimeter have newsboy caps. And, as the featured model in the shots,

Walter Thornton is the only man in the foreground to be sporting a confidently cocked derby. His ears do, in fact, appear "perfectly pinned on."

However and whenever the manufacture of the sign on the photo happened, Walter Thornton has officially entered the world consciousness as the avatar for American bankruptcy. He's literally the "poster boy" for financial disaster, as one can currently purchase either/both of the images, in any size, framed or unframed, at Walmart.com. Their website even offers helpful photographic suggestions as to how they think it might look when hanging over your sofa.

Trying to get the legal records of our father's 1954 kangaroo-court trial unsealed was a lesson in frustration. When the case against our father was eventually thrown out, as per our 2021 query with Queens County Court, the records were sealed and presumably destroyed. We have to accept that as the truth—though we still hold onto a minuscule hope of somehow gaining access to our father's trial transcripts, as well as Quinn's preposterously false dossier of "evidence" against Walter Thornton. We would also love to read the transcriptions of the supposed "hundreds of hours of wiretap evidence," when the Thornton Agency's phones were allegedly placed under FBI surveillance, but we knew that wouldn't be happening since it's hugely unlikely the tapes ever existed to begin with. It was all for show. Simply linking "Walter Thornton" and "Undercover Surveillance" in a tabloid headline was a surefire way to sell newspapers.

Nancy and I have often wondered aloud what our father would have made of the whole "bankrupt investor" thing, were he somehow still alive. We're both convinced that he'd have been outraged at the injustice of this libelously inaccurate portrayal of him. One thing we're fairly certain of: He would have fought back. He would not have let the internet have its way with his image. He certainly would have spoken up.

Nancy and I had finally reached a consensus opinion on what we thought was the real story behind "bankrupt investor" Walter Thornton. We scheduled what we called our "summit"—wherein the two of us would compile all our evidence and finally reach some solid conclusions on everything we'd uncovered. After seventeen years of deep research following our first spotting of the car image in *Seabiscuit*, we'd come to several fairly confident findings.

In some instances, ours is a circumstantial case, as we haven't yet found a "smoking gun" like a retoucher's etching stylus, with the initials *TVQ* on it, or anything like that. But once we realized all signs were pointing toward...the signs, it's been clear enough for us to conclude that the images were doctored; *specifically* doctored to paint our father in a negative light as a lifelong, illegitimate, irresponsible businessman. Designed for maximum shame value. After examining every other possible scenario, it's the only one that seems to make sense.

"*It would have been as simple as Quinn telling Kerwick, 'Find me photos of Walter Thornton that we can dummy-up, kinda like the way we did with the fingerprint records to make him out as that John Hammond robber kid,*'" Nancy said to me, using sort of a film noir lingo. At that point, we had both studied a *lot* of film noir and would slip unavoidably into the dialect in our own conversations. "*Kerwick knows-a-guy-who-knows-a-guy at the Powers Agency, who gives them two modeling shots from 1929 for a photo retoucher to add the '$100 WILL BUY THIS CAR' sign,*" Nancy offered.

"*If that was the case, how did these doctored photos ever end up in the public eye?*" I asked. "*I've given that a lot of thought, even though we don't have the evidence to prove it,*" she explained. "*I think Quinn shared the images with various newspaper editors during the Child Model Racket Trial. Probably with a lot of other smear-campaign stuff, to be systematically doled out, keeping the story alive. And then, all of a sudden, the case is dismissed and the unused materials go into the press's 'photo morgue files'. And then, decades later, a writer or researcher stumbled on them while searching photo archives and mistook them to be literal images. That's my theory, anyway."*

We figure that our father's name was probably written or printed on the back of one or both of the photos, because if these photos were doctored, whoever did so wanted to make sure everyone knew the name of the guy in the center. The lengths to which Quinn/Kerwick went in concocting a Queens-based trial against a man who neither resided in nor had a business in Queens was no less than astounding to begin with. Quinn was a desperate man, with no known lowest threshold in destroying lives. He was trapped; trapped like a rat.

It's unlikely we'll ever know the definitive answer, but this chain of events is not only satisfying to us, but also completely plausible. We're under no illusion that we can completely turn the tide of opinion regarding these photos or our father, but we will continue to try. We never set out to correct history—but once we'd learned the full scope of our father's life and career, we didn't have a choice. We needed to speak up on behalf of our late father because...well, that's just what you do.

In 1955, in the aftermath of his front-page takedown, Walter Thornton announced in Earl Wilson's syndicated Broadway column that he was currently at work on writing his autobiography, "including a chapter on his recent trials and tribulations." It was to be called *The Merchant of Venus.* The book was never published, or, possibly, never even written. And if he did write it, it was lost to history, as we've only found references to it and have never found a manuscript. But we would like to think we picked up the proverbial quill where our father left off...

Epilogue

Nancy/Adriana

Re-framed

Some people are born lucky. Others manage to ride the winds of change and transform themselves, even in circumstances that would spell failure to most. We still marvel at our dad's ability to land on his feet. He survived as an orphan and built the first agency for photographic models and took it from nothing to the top. Even the trial and media scandal did not destroy him.

Not everyone gets the chance for a fresh start. Media scandals have brought down thousands over the past century, and most victims fall into obscurity or disgrace. But a few, whether through good fortune or not, find a new kind of success. For Walter Thornton, starting over ushered in what may have been the happiest season of his life. He had sold his New York interests, but the Canadian Walter Thornton schools that debuted in 1948 had survived the media scandal with no apparent harm.

By 1967 he had transferred most of the management to others. Then his interests lay in his family. With his children Walter was relaxed and animated, telling them funny stories and walking them a mile to and from school each day, accompanied by the family dog and cat. Much of his advice centered on kindness. He talked about his orphan days, and occasionally some other stories about his past, most of which we didn't comprehend. Looking back, though, perhaps it was us who had just missed the clues.

He was easygoing and had a good sense of humor. But if you served yourself a heaping plate at dinner, you had better eat it all! He remembered what it was like to go hungry. Despite his history as a beauty expert and former Miss America judge, he never advised his daughters on beauty or fashion. Now the family home in Ajijic stands as a monument to Walter's creativity. It has become somewhat of a landmark in the area, though he never intended it as more than a gift for the love of his life. When he wasn't working on the house, Walter would enjoy long walks with his family into town or up into the mountains near the bay. Sometimes when he needed space to think, he would walk alone up the mountain path behind the house. Despite his health, he was more active than he must ever have been in his penthouse life in New York City. And if he missed his old life, he certainly never showed it.

Even a short trip into town meant he would come home with something for his children, like our favorite chocolate cakes (*gansitos*). He was a special man who lived in the hearts of many people, but most of all his wife and children. Walter Thornton passed away the morning of May 14, 1990, at age eighty-seven. Dad had started having a series of strokes, so Mom took him to the Veterans Administration Hospital in Long Beach, CA.

He passed away a few days after being admitted, and his sudden death was a shock to us, even though he was older. We arranged a small funeral just for the close family, including his seven children, some grandchildren, and Mom. Because of his military service, he was entitled to a military funeral and burial in the United States. He was laid to rest at Riverside National Cemetery in Riverside, CA. This cemetery is specifically for military veterans and personnel. He was honored with a complete U.S. Army Veteran's tribute, recognizing his service during World War One and his contributions in World War Two.

We have thought of him every day since then. Many times, while working on this book, we wished our father could be sitting next to us, answering all the questions we never realized we had. We wanted to know more about his life before he became famous, as well as about his brothers and sisters. Additionally, we have many questions about his professional life in New York. How did he adjust after the trial? We're also curious about what happened to the rest of his archives: model photos, letters, and the like. How did so many of his archives end up in the marketplace or in different libraries? What is the story behind the 'bankrupt investor' photos? There are so many more questions we wish we could ask him.

After all we learned, we finally landed on a sort of compromise for us to be able to still embrace the car photos, even though we were now fully aware that they hardly portrayed a happy image of our father. But we realized, like it or not, real or fake, they are a big part of our lives. We sent a large, digital copy of the group image to a photo-editing expert in New York, to have the sign removed—"restored," if you will. We had a movie-poster-sized copy of the amended photo printed and had it framed and hung in the castle. We think this will help bring some peace to our father's still-benevolently restless spirit, to finally have that doctored "bankrupt investor" image removed from his castle, once and for all.

But most of all, we wish we could tell him that his story is being told. He got his book! And he is going to be where he belongs in history.

About the Authors

Walter Thornton's daughters have devoted countless years to researching, writing, and archiving their father's extensive collection of photos and documents, discovered in the attic of their childhood home. Drawing upon the invaluable insights collected from their father's documents and aided by the assistance of numerous librarians from esteemed institutions such as the Library of Congress, the New York Public Library, and others across the country, as well as historians, they have fully immersed themselves in the quest to unveil their father's narrative.

Nancy Thornton Navarro (L) is a former trademark and copyright attorney who has also served as the Chairman of the Board of Directors for the Irving, Texas Hispanic Chamber of Commerce. Nancy currently lives near Dallas with her husband and is a proud mother of three.

Adriana Thornton-Cornejo (R) is a Programmer, 2D Artist, and CAD Drafter at Focus 360, a company serving the Home Building Industry. Adriana hopes that, with renewed public interest in her father's life and career, she can one day open a Walter Thornton Museum. She lives near Los Angeles with her husband and their two sons.

Philip Mershon is an entertainment industry historian and storyteller who loves going down a good rabbit hole in search of the truth. He lives in Palm Springs, California.

Selected Bibliography

"Actress Plans Modeling Agency." *Elmira Star-Gazette*. May 9, 1946.

"Ohio Roster of Soldiers, Sailors, and Marines in World War I, 1917-1918." Ancestry.com.

1930 Knapp Felt Hats Ad ~ Percy Edward Anderson, Vintage Clothing & Accessory. *Attic Paper*. April 3, 1930. https://www.atticpaper.com/proddetail.php?prod=1930-knapp-felt-hats-ad-harwood. Accessed April 4, 2023.

"Army Sweetheart." *Highland Park Post-Dispatch*, May 21, 1942.

Bacall, Lauren. *Lauren Bacall By Myself*. 1985. Ballantine Books.

"Broadway's Answer to Hollywood." *The Free Lance-Star*. April 4, 1941. https://news.google.com/newspapers?nid=1298&dat=19410404&id=Pg4TAAAAIBAJ&sjid=OOQDAAAAIBAJ&pg=6996,4901232&hl=en. Accessed April 7, 2023.

Brown, Gordon. "Anything to Make the Soldier Ladies Happy." *New York Post*. December 19, 1940.

"*Jerry Cooper Outstanding Diamond Recording Get a Pin-Up Girl.*" *World Radio History*. April 17, 1948. https://worldradiohistory.com/Archive-All-Music/Billboard/40s/1948/Billboard%201948-04-17.pdf. Accessed April 9, 2023.

Carnegie, Dale. "Author of "How to Win Friends and Influence People." *The Pittsburgh Press*. December 26, 1940.https://news.google.com/newspapers?nid=1144&dat=19401226&i

d=k3EbAAAAIBAJ&sjid=X0wEAAAAIBAJ&pg=2392,4152633&hl=en. Accessed April 4, 2023.

Clark, Betty. "Model Wife Says Anyone Can Keep Spouse Charmed." *St. Petersburg Times.* June 3, 1945.https://news.google.com/newspapers?nid=888&dat=19450603&id =FkdPAAAAIBAJ&sjid=0U4DAAAAIBAJ&pg=4522,4850118&hl=en. Accessed 9, 2023.

Dickson, Paul. *War Slang.* 2004. Brassey's Inc.

Arnold, Elliott. "Now, I'll Tell You About It, Says Sue Hayward, Smiling." *World Telegram.* October 24, 1929.

Evans-Smith, Eileen. "Person to Person: Every Girl a Model?" *Ottawa Citizen.* November 13, 1962. https://news.google.com/newspapers?nid=2194&dat=19621113&id=hFU lAAAAIBAJ&sjid=ieUFAAAAIBAJ&pg=4302,3069328&hl=en. Accessed April 9, 2023.

"Knapp-felt 1920s USA Men's Hats by The Advertising Archives." *Fine Art America.* April 16, 2013. https://fineartamerica.com/feature d/knapp-felt-1920s-usa-mens-hats-the-advertising-archives.html. Accessed April 4, 2023.

Millstein, Gilbert. "The Modeling Business." *LIFE Magazine.* March 25, 1946.

"Jack Sutter Case Histories in Photography Racket in Rockland County Disclosed by Skahen." *The Journal News.* September 4, 1953.

"Beautiful Models? Yes, and Now They're Insured." *The Journal News.* February 1, 1940.

Lacey, Robert. "Model Woman." *Google Books.* HarperCollins. June 16, 2015. https://www.google.com/books/edition/Model_Woman/X6qkBQAAQ BAJ?hl=en&gbpv=1&dq=almost+all+the+girls+that+appeared+in+ads+an d+magazines+were+from+the+Walter+Thornton+Model+Agency*&pg= PT14&printsec=frontcover#v=onepage&q=almost%20all%20the%20gi rls%20that%20ap. Accessed April 9, 2023.

LaGuardia, Robert, and Auceri, Gene. *Red: The Tempestuous Life of Susan Hayward.* Robson Books. January 1, 1986.

Lait, Jack. "Highlights of Broadway From the Circle to the Square." *Albuquerque Journal*. October 4, 1931.

"Men's Lady." *The Spokesman-Review*. June 26, 1947. https://news.google.com/newspapers?nid=1314&dat=19470126&id=MF 0zAAAAIBAJ&sjid=ReUDAAAAIBAJ&pg=3289,3630067&hl=en. Accessed April 7, 2023.

Millstein, Gilbert. "The Modeling Business." *LIFE Magazine*. March 25, 1946. https://books.google.com/books?id=iEgEAAAAMBAJ&q=LIFE+Mar+2 5,+1946#v=onepage&q=LIFE%20Mar%2025%2C%201946&f=false. Accessed April 6, 2023.

"Miss America 1933." *Wikipedia*, https://en.wikipedia.org/wiki/Miss _America_1933. Accessed April 9, 2023.

"Million Dollars' Worth of Beauty Insured." *The Daily Notes*. January 27, 1940.

"Modeling Career No Picnic Eager Parents Are Warned." *Dayton Daily News*. August 10, 1949.

Evans-Smith, Eileen. "Every Girl a Model?" *Ottawa Citizen*. November 13, 1962. https://news.google.com/newspapers?nid=2194&dat=19621113&id=hFU lAAAAIBAJ&sjid=ieUFAAAAIBAJ&pg=4302,3069328&hl=en. Accessed April 4, 2023.

"A Real PINUP." *Herald and Review*. May 9, 1948.https://www.new spapers.com/newspage/88460118/. Accessed April 7, 2023.

"Bricklayer Parks Trowel: Emerges as Glorified Youth of Collar Ads." *The Minneapolis Sunday Tribune*. August 10, 1930. https://www.news papers.com/clip/89825834/bricklayer-parks-trowel/. Accessed April 4, 2023.

"Publicity photographs of Walter Thornton - NYPL Digital Collections." *NYPL Digital Collections*. January 1927. https://digitalcollecti ons.nypl.org/items/3053a750-52be-0135-513f-318e59ba1814. Accessed April 4, 2023.

"Pin-Up Comes to Life." *India-Burma Theater Roundup*. January 3, 1946. http://www.cbi-theater.com/roundup/roundup010346.html. Accessed April 9, 2023.

"Photogenic Youngsters In Demand As Models In Postwar Advertising Trend." *The Owensboro Messenger*. May 13, 1948.

Crowther III, Samuel. "300 Models, No Job: Thornton Aide Tells of Failure." *New York Journal-American*. January 26, 1954.

Reichley, Morris. "Like An Arabian Circus." *Chapala*. March 2014. https://chapala.com/elojo/162-articles-2014/march-2014/2423-like-an-arabian-circus. Accessed March 26, 2023.

"Sued for 'Forgetting'." *The Michigan Daily*. August 5, 1939. https://digital.bentley.umich.edu/midaily/mdp.39015071756600/151

Swan, Gilbert. "Yes, Walter Thornton Uses His Head to Good Advantage, for He Has the Most Demanded Cranium of Any Male Model". *Star-Gazette*. January 26, 1931. Accessed April 4, 2023.

"Starr Faitfull Cremation Halted." *Daily News*. June 12, 1931.

"Pin up Polka." *Billboard*. February 21, 1948. https://worldradiohistory.com/Archive-All-Music/Billboard/50s/1952/Billboard%201952-02-21.pdf. Accessed April 9, 2023.

Billboard. August 7, 1948. https://worldradiohistory.com/Archive-All-Music/Billboard/40s/1948/Billboard%201948-08-07.pdf. Accessed April 9, 2023.

The Encyclopedia of Television Shows. https://www.google.com/books/edition/Encyclopedia_of_Television_Shows_1925_th/YX_daEhlnbsC?hl=en&gbpv=1&dq=Louise+Arnold**walter+thornton&pg=PA1076&printsec=frontcover.Accessed April 7, 2023.

"Walter Thornton, Agent for Models, Dies of Stroke at 88 (Published 1990)." *The New York Times*. May 16, 1990. https://www.nytimes.com/1990/05/16/obituaries/walter-thornton-agent-for-models-dies-of-stroke-at-88.html. Accessed April 4, 2023.

"Thornton is free in model 'racket." *The New York Times*. June 3, 1954. https://www.nytimes.com/1954/06/03/archives/thornton-is-free-in-model-racket.html. Accessed March 26, 2023.

Rowan, Terry. *World War II Goes to the Movies & Television Guide.* Lulu.com, 2012.

Thornton Walter Agency Ad. *The Brooklyn Daily Eagle.* October 4, 1944.

"You Too, Can Be Beautiful." *The New True Story Magazine.* January 1940.

"The Merchant of Venus." *The Saturday Evening Post.* October 30, 1937.

"Trials of a Merchant of Venus." *El Paso Times.* July 26, 1936.

Erickson, Wendell. "Four Years Is Usually the Limit of Artists' Model's Career." *The Des Moines Register.* December 1, 1935.

Leigh, Wendy. *True Grace: The Life and Times of an American Princess.* St. Martin's Griffin. 2007.

"Our Most Glamorous Models Fade Out After 2 Years." *The Courier-Journal.* October 14, 1934. "$600,00 Losses Bared: Alleged Model Racket Fleeces Proud Parents." *Oakland Tribune.* January 26, 1954.

"Miss America 1933." Wikipedia. March 30, 2023. https://en.wikipedia.org/wiki/Miss_America_1933. Accessed April 4, 2023.

LETTERS:
Letter written on June 14, 1946, by Walter Thornton to Mr. M.D. Clofine, of *News of the Day.*

Letter from Arlene Dahl to the Thornton sisters dated 2022.

Letter from First Lieutenant (retired) Eric Johnson of Forensic Photo Analysis Services dated 2021.

INTERVIEWS:
Candelaria Thornton

Myra Dolan

Kirby Kooluris

Milton Keynes UK
Ingram Content Group UK Ltd.
UKHW052309280324
440326UK00007B/157/J